This book is so poignant and relevant for such a time as this! Luanne Botta writes honestly, practically, and sensitively. Young hearts will definitely be challenged and motivated to lead pure lives because of the loving and powerful challenge that Luanne offers them.

Kathy Troccoli
Singer, Speaker, Author

Luanne's ability to present God's truth with her energy and passion is a dynamite package! She is definitely an expert in her field.

Deb Ott
Leadership Director, Silver Ring Thing (2000-2007)

Luanne Botta is on the cutting edge of a timely and timeless issue relevant to all teenagers and their families and to our society as a whole. Others have addressed the issue of sexual abstinence outside of the marriage covenant but not always with the anointing, zeal and compassion that allows Luanne to touch and equip our young people so effectively.

Rev. Gary Mitrik
Senior Pastor, Greater Works Outreach
Monroeville, Pennsylvania

As a Christian school administrator for nineteen years, I clearly understood the need for giving young people information from a biblical perspective. We live in a world where unlimited information can be obtained at the touch of a key. Our teens are flooded with messages and images from the prevalent ungodly, secular view of this culture. As Christian educators, we are completely remiss if we do not provide them with God's truth concerning their sexuality and life choices. The information must be biblically based and the informer must be spiritually grounded and motivated. I find these both to be true of Luanne and this curriculum.

Sharon L. Herbster
Administrator, Christian Fellowship Academy (1989-2008)

A truly Godly minister is created by God and is a gift to the Church. Luanne Botta is one of these ministers. Luanne is anointed and called by God with a message that is timeless. The message that she teaches about knowing God and walking with Him in holiness and truth has been proven to resonate with the young people of each generation. I have had both the privilege of hearing and working alongside Luanne. I have seen the Spirit of God supply the words and move through her ministry and dramatically transform the lives and hearts of young people. If you are serious about seeing the lives of your young people changed and their lives redirected, it is imperative that you expose them to the message Luanne carries and her curriculum "Young Hearts. Pure Lives."

Richard M. Nugara, Ph.D.
Adjunct Professor of Religion and Philosophy, Regent University

Our culture is in great need of filling the minds of our young people with God's philosophy of life. Luanne – an excellent example of a Godly woman – has done this in her book, "Young Hearts. Pure Lives." This book is the result of many years of using the principles in the laboratory of life and seeing the practical results. These are not just ideas that should be effective – they have been proven in reality. Knowing Luanne and seeing the outcomes firsthand allow me to recommend it highly.

R. L. Malamisuro
Director/Founder, Grace Ministries, Inc.

I have had the pleasure of knowing Luanne Botta on a professional and personal level. Luanne has been drawn into a unique and very important ministry: preaching and teaching abstinence. This subject is not always readily accepted but nevertheless is supported by Scripture and the teaching of our Lord Jesus Christ. In her curriculum "Young Hearts. Pure Lives," Luanne approaches the subject of purity by being "wise as a serpent, gentle as a dove." I have personally seen the far-reaching positive effects that her abstinence program has had on the lives of many young people as well as on entire families. She is unwavering in her convictions yet never condemning. Very few people have the conviction, boldness and burning desire to make this all-important message a ministry.

Vera Marelli
Program Director, Tickets for Kids Charities

I have known Miss Botta for 14 years as a teacher, leader, friend and ministry partner. She is a dynamic woman whose passion is to see God's people grow in their understanding of His plan for their lives. Her attention grabbing, "from the heart" presentation, draws people from where they live and leads them to a better place. She was an involved and influential teacher who had a heart for so many of her students. I find that my ability to describe the impact her ministry has had on lives is lacking. It is my hope that you would be able to invite this ministry into the lives of your students so that they too can experience the transforming message for their own lives.

Rev. Jonathan Curry
Children's Pastor, Greater Works Outreach
Monroeville, Pennsylvania

Young Hearts.
Pure Lives.

A Biblically based
abstinence education program.

Young Hearts. Pure Lives.

Staying Pure in a Reckless World

Luanne Botta

ISBN: 978-1-60374-260-3
Printed in the U.S.A.
Copyright © 2010 by Luanne Botta

Published by
Whitaker House
1030 Hunt Valley Circle
New Kensington, PA 15068

Edited by Vicki Mlinar and Jenni Miller

www.luannebotta.com

Dedicated to my mom and dad.

After watching your marriage of 58 years and counting...
you have taught me that love, complete commitment,
faithfulness, family, laughter and the love of Jesus Christ
keeps a marriage strong. What an inheritance
you have given! I love you!

Special thank you to Dr. Angela R. Anderson.

I would never have tackled this endeavor without you.
Your encouragement, professional insight and input,
and your treasured friendship have been such a blessing to
me. Those late nights with two babies at our feet
and one in your arms were priceless for both of us!
Thanks for believing with me in encouraging this generation
to stay pure in a reckless world!

Forward

I met Luanne Botta my junior year of high school. She was my volleyball coach and gym teacher. She was a woman on fire for the Lord who truly cared about my heart and my spiritual life (not to mention my volleyball stats☺). The second semester of our junior year, our Bible class was put on hold while Miss Botta came into the class for nine weeks to teach us about abstinence and purity.

As a young woman who had not heard about intimacy from this perspective before, I was floored. I can remember asking so many questions, cracking jokes and disrupting class – only to sit at home later and digest it all. I still remember the tune that I used to remember the scripture, "All other sins a man commits are outside his body, but he who sins sexually sins against his own body." Okay, it may have been more of a "rap" than a tune… but it is still stuck in my head nonetheless. Her words cut to my core. She challenged me as a student in high school to consider God's plan for me, to be proactive about my relationship with my boyfriend and to keep my head and heart in the Word.

My husband and I dated for 6 years before we got married. I am positive we would not have been able to remain pure without the instruction that we received during high school regarding purity.

Sitting as a student in Luanne's class years ago, I would have never imagined that my educational pursuits would bring us together on this subject again. Having taught at both the high school and college level, I am well aware that the battle for young women to remain pure rages on daily. For years, I have encouraged Luanne to put the

Godly advice and wisdom that she has taught to so many students into book form. When she finally approached me last spring to assist her in creating this curriculum, I was honored.

Luanne's vast experience in teaching the Word to different audiences and in classrooms across the country makes her lessons engaging and poignant. She has been in ministry for over 20 years and continues to encourage and inspire both students and adults alike. Her great and abiding passion is to meet students where they are and inspire them to recognize that God's plan is bigger than they could ever imagine.

This course will not only open your eyes to all that God has in-store for your life, but also show you the reality of the world in which you currently live. The timeless truths Luanne shares in both the videos and the book are as relevant today as they were to me years ago. I am certain that these lessons will be shared with my daughter in the coming years, as we strive to teach her to live pure in a reckless world.

Dr. Angela R. Anderson

Contents

Terms and Definitions

Abstain—to refrain from something; to hold back.

Adultery—voluntary sexual intercourse with another person other than your spouse.

Celibacy—the state of not being married; abstaining from sexual intercourse.

Character—qualities or features that distinguish one person from another; moral ethical strength; reputation.

Desensitized—non-reactive; insensitive, callous, numb.

Fornication—consensual sexual intercourse between two persons not married to each other.

Illicit—not permitted, unlawful.

Immoral—conscienceless of moral principals; what is right.

Innuendo—to hint, allusion, insinuation, not straight forward.

Integrity—honest, high standards of morals and values.

Moral—capable of making the distinction between right and wrong in conduct.

Promiscuous—sexual intercourse with many persons, without plan or purpose; casual.

Respect—to consider worthy of high regard; held in honor or high esteem.

Responsible—accountable; obligation.

Virtuous—moral excellence; value; right action and thinking.

Introduction

T his program was written to you out of a heart of compassion for this generation of Christian teenage girls to know the truth about love, sex and purity **God's way**!

I was a teacher at a private Christian school for 16 years and after the second week I was there a senior girl came up to me and told me she was having sex with her boyfriend and didn't want to do it anymore. From that day on, through those 16 years, my office door was like a revolving door with one girl after another sharing heartache after heartache over this one subject…<u>sex outside of marriage</u>. I use to think that if the walls in my office could speak they would cry over all I was hearing from so many girls and all the tears that were shed because of the boundaries that were crossed in this area of sexuality.

I know this subject of "staying pure in a reckless world" is not very popular in our society. In fact, the world screams at you to bow to their view on sex, which has caused nothing but heartache and brokenness of spirit and emotions. God has such a better way. And I feel His voice has gotten lost in the midst of so much confusion.

I know I may step on a few toes through this study, but it is to be honest with you about where you might be heading in your life— places that are not good for you. I know some of you may have already fallen to sexual sin and you need a safe place to start again. God's mercy and goodness is there for you! You will see how much He loves you and is waiting for you to start again! Others of you are standing in great courage, waiting on the Lord from a clean, pure heart…oh how He loves all of you so!

The intention of this program is not just to prevent pregnancy or sexually transmitted diseases, but to enhance the true understanding that you are loved, accepted and treasured by your Heavenly Father! Building you up with truth, encouraging you to stand, challenging you to stand alone if you must is crucial to your growth and victory in this area of sexual purity.

Please take every opportunity through the workbook, the homework available and your in class activities to get a better understanding of the truths that are conveyed to you through this study. I pray your heart will beat for the truth of God's Word. Hopefully there is enough information here to help you walk out this life of purity until you say "I do" at the altar!

*Ladies, start today...make a commitment
to become a pure woman of God!*

"Watch over your heart with all diligence, for from it flow the springs of life." (Proverbs 4:23 NASB)

Chapter 1

God Has a Plan

"I have loved you with an everlasting love; therefore I have drawn you with lovingkindness." Jeremiah 31:3 NASB

I want all of you to truly understand that God is *for* relationships! They were His idea from the start! He wanted a relationship, a family, with His children, and He knows best how to create relationships for each one of us here on earth.

Some of you will marry one day and some of you will decide not to. Both plans are good, when the plans are God's! Because premarital sex is so out of control in our society today, it is used haphazardly, and treated more like a joke than as a physical, emotional, spiritual, and mental commitment to another person before God.

I want you to know that God is all for sex! He had a plan from the very beginning concerning sex, and His plan was <u>solely</u> in the context of marriage. Outside of marriage, sex is disastrous, causing broken hearts, shattered relationships, insecurity, disease, emotional heartache, and broken fellowship from the very heart of God.

Marriage is a gift from God! It is a gift that He designed to bring the greatest fulfillment in a relationship here on earth between one man and one woman! This gift of marriage is to be:

- **treasured.** *"He who finds a wife, finds a good thing and obtains favor from the Lord."* (Proverbs 18:22 NASB)

- **protected.** *"Husbands, love your wives, just as Christ also loved the church and gave Himself up for her."* (Ephesians 5:25 NASB)

- **enjoyed.** *"This is my beloved, and this is my friend."* (Song of Solomon 5:16 NASB)

- **held with great commitment.** *"Let the marriage bed be held in honor amongst all, and the marriage bed be undefiled."* (Hebrews 13:4 NASB)

- **handled with the Word of God and His guidelines throughout it all.** *"For I hate divorce, says the Lord, the God of Israel…so take heed to your spirit, that you do not deal treacherously."* (Malachi 2:16 NASB)

You see, God has the *best* plan concerning relationships and sex. Through this study, please embrace His truths and allow His Holy Spirit to reprogram your mind away from what the world is conveying to you about sex and relationships. Then you will be more than satisfied when the time comes for you to commit yourself to singleness or to the man God has for you. In God's plans, you can't lose: He works things out for your good and His glory!

SINCE THE BEGINNING OF TIME

It has been God's heart since the beginning of time to have an intimate, personal relationship with His children. To love, protect, and provide for them.

In the second chapter of Genesis, life in the Garden was good! Adam and Eve could eat freely from all God had given them. In that freedom, there was pure love, contentment, joy, no fear, great peace, oneness with God, laughter, rest, no anxiety…the list could go on and on! Obedience to what God says leads to life!

> Obedience to what God says leads to life!

God made a covenant, a binding agreement, a promise that maintained a relationship with Adam and Eve (and with you.) In that covenant, He claimed them as His own. They were His children in His image. He promised never to leave or forsake them, and He promised to be their God. He never wanted that relationship to be broken or hindered in any way. But in their disobedience, Adam and Eve insisted on listening to the voice of Satan and his accusations against what God had clearly said. Then emotional, physical, and spiritual death entered the world.

God wants you to enjoy the life that He has given you here on earth. He wants you to walk in the gifts and relationships He places before you.

You must be very wise to the voices of opposition that are contrary to what God is saying. This is especially vital when dealing with relationships.

Let's go further.

CONSEQUENCES OF DISOBEDIENCE

In the third chapter of Genesis, Satan denied that which God called good, questioning the truthfulness of His Word. We must understand Satan's way of deception that Eve missed here.

It says in Genesis 3:6, "When the woman saw that the fruit of the tree was good and pleasing to the eye, and also desirable for gaining wisdom, she took and ate." Notice – she saw, she took, and she ate. After reasoning with the voice of deception in her mind, she decided to reach out and grab the lie, taste, and eat.

You might think, "How stupid, Eve, God had given you so much!" All He asked them not to touch was that one tree. But think about it, God has given you so much as well! He wants you to grow up whole and healthy, without insecurity, fears, or rejection regarding relationships. He's asked you not to defile yourself before marriage, and yet look around to your generation…they see, they take, and they eat anyhow.

How is this any different from what Adam and Eve did? Think about that. Because of this disobedience, and just as God had warned, sin and the consequences of sin entered the world.

SPIRITUAL BROKENNESS

You need to understand—and maybe some of you are experiencing this right now—sex is not just physical but emotional, mental, and spiritual. We forget that spiritual death can occur when we are walking in disobedience to God's will. There may be nothing that lays more heavily on us than when we are in Christ but feel the depth of a separation in that relationship.

Sin many times causes us to withdrawal from God. You can allow your thoughts to be so riddled with lust, impure motives, impure thoughts, so over-saturated with romantic movies and books with sexual scenes and content that your mind becomes tainted and unclean. This causes a breach between you and God.

Spiritual brokenness brings about not only a broken relationship with God but the loss of one's ability and desire to please or seek Him. This can cause you to do your own thing and live in the wilderness of broken fellowship with God. It's not that He has left you, but the sin you carry has caused a breach between the two of you. Don't let your heart be imprisoned to this kind of disobedience. He is calling you back to Himself.

GOD OUR RESCUER

God has come to rescue His own. All that was once made so perfect in the Garden has become tainted. Because God loves, accepts, cherishes, and has made a covenant with you, He hasn't left you in this state of sin. His mercy and His Father's heart toward you has once and for all rescued you from eternal sin and death through the sacrifice and the shedding of the blood of His own Son, Jesus Christ. Through Jesus' resurrection, you are free to go to Him and be renewed; the separation or breach in relationship is completely gone through true repentance and forgiveness. He calls you His Bride. "For the wedding of the Lamb has come, and His bride has made herself ready." (Revelations 19:7)

What great news to know that you have been rescued! And what a great Warrior your true Bridegroom really is!

This is why you need to adhere to what you learn in this study of God's plan for your life regarding relationships and sex. There is so much involved. It's about valuing and respecting your body. It's about desiring to be whole in Christ long before you go looking for love. It's about being confident in who you are and Whose you are! You want His best…His timing!

He is completely for you. You are always on His heart and mind! And He wants you to see His heart in this matter regarding sexual purity and His plans for you.

Below are some truths to help you solidify that relationships were God's idea from the start and He had you in mind when He spoke these words of truth!

MAKING GOD'S CASE THROUGH HIS WORD

"For I know the plans I have for you, declares the Lord, plans to prosper you and not to harm you. Plans to give you a future and a hope."   —Jeremiah 29:11

I know all of you are very familiar with this verse, but read it again.

This is a very personal Scripture. Do you see how God says, "I know," "I have," and "for you"? Do you believe He has a plan for your life? Does God have good or bad plans? Is His future for you a disaster, or one full of hope?

You must rest assured that God has had your days written down before even one of them came to be (see Psalm 139:16). Trust Him through this time of decisions: what friends (guys and girls) you are to link arms with; where to go to college; what career/ministry you should pursue. Pray for your husband and ask God to bring you together. He has the plan, and He wants to reveal it to you piece by piece. Take the time to sit before Him and begin to listen for direction, guidance, and for all He has in store. His plans are good: to bring you a bright future filled with great hope!

"There is an appointed time for everything. And there is a time for every event under heaven…"
—Ecclesiastes 3:1 NASB

There absolutely is a time and season for everything in life. If you push for *your* timetable, instead of God's, on events in your life, you can cause real havoc in your life.

It's not necessary to chase after boys! God brought Eve to Adam. The timing for each of you in this area will be different. Allow God to work things out for you in His way and His time. You will see that He always knows exactly what He is doing!

Listen carefully: the word "time" in this Scripture means "divinely appointed"! So, if you let Him, God will divinely appoint the time and the man you are to marry. He'll make the meeting with this young man a great gift and a wonderful surprise! Waiting on that time frame is what makes things difficult. We will deal with waiting in another chapter, but when you are confident that God has a divinely appointed time, it will allow you not to sit around waiting, but remain very active in what is in front of you now.

"Daughters of Jerusalem, I charge you...do not arouse or awaken love until it so desires."—Song of Solomon 2:7

This scripture is repeated two other times in the Song of Solomon (3:5 and 8:4), and it is always in the context of physical intimacy. It is a charge and a challenge to you as daughters of the King! It is saying loud and clear – don't arouse love or awaken love until the proper time.

> **Feelings aren't enough to support a lasting relationship.**

Many young people interpret their strong emotional feelings for someone as love, not understanding that feelings aren't enough to support a lasting relationship let alone a marriage. When you arouse or awaken the physical part of a relationship, it will cause you to make unwise decisions that your flesh and feelings can't handle.

You are being charged and challenged today to walk with integrity in your relationship with boys and not awaken desire that should not be fulfilled outside the marriage bed. Ladies, you are looking to stay pure in a reckless world. It's going to take great discipline and sacrifice on your part in this season of your life *until*—and I repeat, *until*—the proper time has been divinely ordained by the Lord!

"For this is the will of God, your sanctification; that is that you abstain from sexual immorality; that each of you know how to possess his own vessel in sanctification and honor, not in lustful passion, like the Gentiles who do not know God; and that no man transgress and defraud his brother in the matter because the Lord is the avenger in all these things, just as we also told you before and solemnly warned you. For God has not called us for the purpose of impurity, but in sanctification. Consequently, he who rejects this is not

rejecting man but the God who gives His Holy Spirit to you."
—1 Thessalonians 4:3-8 NASB

Everyone wants to know what the will of God is. It is always such a popular question. When it comes to sexual purity, God's will is written out so clearly in this Scripture. In fact, it gives you the exact answer: abstain from sexual immorality! It can't get any clearer than that!

You need to know how to possess and honor your own body. Not in lustful passion as is portrayed so much in the media. Your body is not to be used or freely given away. When you committed your heart to the Lord, you became His. Now your body is the temple of the Holy Spirit who is in you, and you are not your own! It is to your benefit and your blessing that you know how to protect and treasure your body. That is what the Lord is clearly trying to say here.

This Scripture also says not to defraud your brother in the matter. Defraud in this context means "take advantage of." It is not the will of God for you to take advantage of a guy by the way you dress, or to choose to offer parts of your body to him in any manner. Look carefully at the last line. To reject this truth is not rejecting man, but rejecting God and His will for your life.

Wow! Is all this more than you bargained for? I sure hope not! There is a lot to ponder and take to the Lord in prayer. He wants the best for you. That's why He gives you direct answers to this question of His will for your life! He loves you—so listen to Him.

"Flee from sexual immorality. All other sins a man commits are outside his body, but he who sins sexually sins against his own body."—1 Corinthians 6:18

Flee sexual immorality. Again, another charge! Another challenge! To flee is to *run*. To do a 180-degree turn and run! It is so specific here that those who sin sexually sin against their own bodies. Pretty amazing, isn't it? We do this to ourselves simply because we desire our own way.

Once again, God created sex to be a beautiful and essential part of marriage. Outside of the marriage bed, it always hurts someone. Spiritually, it can affect your walk with the Lord. It can affect you emotionally causing depression and discouragement. Through disease, it most certainly can affect you physically. That's why it says to flee, run from sexual sin.

On TV, in movies, and in music, sex outside of marriage is treated as normal and the family unit is treated as odd. But we all know that sexual sin can devastate families, ministries, nations, and the best of friends. God knows that the consequences of sex outside of marriage are costly, and He desires that we not get caught in the grip of its trap. Trust His truth in this matter!

These are just a few Scriptures to make God's case for His plan for your life. He is for you and not against you. His plans are good! His intention is to bring you joy, hope, and a future!

LOOK ONE MORE TIME!

So you see, ladies, it's time to claim or reclaim your integrity and your relationship with God, even when it is not popular in our culture or among your peers to do so! I trust that, through this study, you will have a new attitude about your value in God, about your body, and about setting boundaries to protect what is yours until the man God has chosen for you commits his life to you at the altar.

I know that waiting until marriage is a very, very unpopular message. But I pray you understand that your worth is far above jewels. Your heart and body are to be respected and treated as valued property of the Lord. You are a gift, a pearl of great price! Your body is not to be given to just anyone to be touched or sampled, but given to that one who knows the cost of real love and commitment. That, my friend, is only found within the marriage vows. To give your heart and body before that time will only open you up to being used, taken advantage of, deceived, and greatly disappointed.

It TAKES the strength and self-control of the Lord within to be willing to wait for the appointed time to awaken love.

Let's start the journey today!

Journal Entry:

Please go to Appendix A in the back of the book, Day One, to complete all questions and journal entries that will help you to think and make the necessary changes in this area of sexual purity.

Assigned Homework:

1. Read the paragraph below in front of the mirror 3 times by yourself **out loud**! Don't read it quietly to yourself...speak it out looking at your face in the mirror! Believe what you are saying about yourself and watch how the Lord will begin to change your mindset and attitude about your self-worth!

   "I am deeply loved, completely forgiven, totally accepted and absolutely complete in Christ! He has chosen me! I am the apple of His eye! He has not forgotten me! His thoughts toward me outnumber the grains of sand! I am beautiful, treasured and set apart! He compares me to no one! I have value, purpose, and a destiny created just for me by God! I belong to Him! He counts every hair on my head and bottles every tear! He is intimately acquainted with every detail of my life! I trust Him! I accept that I am a daughter of the King, and I am to treat myself and be treated as one!" *(Try to do this at least twice a day, every day for at least 3 months for it to go deep in to your heart!)*

2. The way we dress says a lot about who we are. Look through your clothes closet. Journal in the Appendix A section in the back of the workbook on **what signal** you are sending to adults, to your peers, to the opposite sex.

PERSONAL TESTIMONY...
BETTER THAN FAIRYTALES

"He makes all things beautiful in His time..."
—Ecclesiastes 3:11

"Why are you waiting? You are 19 years old and pretty. Why wait for one man? What if he isn't any good and you guys aren't compatible in bed? People are like cars, you have to try them out before you purchase one." These were the questions and arguments I was getting as an enlisted woman in the US Navy. But there was no question in my mind why I was waiting. I never wanted to be married to just anyone, I wanted God's choice for my husband and I knew if I waited on His timing it would be, literally, a match made in heaven.

I remember when I was confronted with those questions and statements I was getting regarding why I was waiting, I often gave the following answers: first there is no perfect condom that protects you against an STD, Aids or pregnancy, only abstinence provides 100% protection. Second, there is no condom that protects your mind from the memories or your heart from hardening from sex with multiple partners. But the most important thing for me was that I really wanted the will of God for my life and was determined to live as He desired even through all of those years of the ups and downs of dating relationships.

Would you believe that God made me wait until I was 33 years old to marry and have sex for the first time? But my prince was well worth it and more than I could ever have imagined! I had other offers of marriage before, but I didn't want to get married just to get married. I wanted what God intended marriage to be.

And may I be honest with you that I realize now how much we rationalize that as long as we aren't having sex we can kiss and fool around with whomever we want. I had earned the nickname kissing bandit in my single years. Unfortunately, it really lessened the value of my kisses. What a great misunderstanding that was for me then as I am in my marriage now and truly know the value of a kiss.

I am glad I waited until I was married but I also want to reassure young woman that being virgins doesn't make a marriage, but what a wonderful foundation and connection it allows you to have with just each other. And may I also assure you God was right all along!! Sex was His idea and when we do things His way, what a blessing and joy He allows it to be!

Tammy

Chapter 2

You Are Worth Waiting For

"Strength and dignity are her clothing and she smiles at the future." —Proverbs 31:25 NASB

How you view yourself will greatly impact how you let others treat you. Low self-image and insecurities plague teenagers in an era where your heroes and role models have to look perfect, have a lot of money, drive a sharp-looking car, have a gorgeous boyfriend, etc. However, your *real* self-worth and value come from truly understanding who you are in the eyes of God (the Audience of One), and how much you are treasured and cared for by Him.

You are very unique, one-of-a-kind to God—the apple of His eye! There are no carbon copies here! He wants you to realize that your value and self-worth come from your relationship with Him first. He honestly wants you to know within your heart that you are deeply loved, completely forgiven, totally accepted, and fully chosen by Him! If you can get this first and foremost in your heart, spirit, and soul, you can begin to understand that relationships with your friends and with the opposite sex are an added bonus to your life; you don't have to try so hard to be accepted by others!

YOU ARE VALUABLE IN HIS EYES

You are worth waiting for! You were never meant to be used, abused, or thrown away. That is not how you were ever intended to be treated! The moment you allow yourself to be taken advantage of out of fear of not being accepted, liked, or "one of the gang," you will lose a great part of who you are and who you are meant to be! When you are certain of your value in God's eyes, strength and dignity will truly be your clothing…and you will smile at the future! (Proverbs 31:25)

God has a good plan and future for your life! You have to believe that. When you get on board with what He has ordained for you, you can relax, and rest in the fact that He is in control of every detail of your life. Every hair of your head is counted. He even knows the ones that come out in your hair brush! He is that aware of your every move, every thought, every heart's desire, and every concern.

Get to know Him first. Truly get to know Him through His Word and by spending quality time in His presence before you embark on relationships of any kind. It will help you to make clear choices for yourself. You won't feel you have to prove yourself to anyone when you are secure in His love for you. HE is your Savior, not your friends or your boyfriend.

> HE is your Savior, not your friends or your boyfriend.

This is the season and time in your life when you need to put attributes of a solid woman of God in place for yourself. You are preparing yourself to be the friend, sister, aunt, wife, and mom you were meant to be. You need a good foundation for building solid Godly relationships! Self-discipline, positive body image, self-respect, love, joy, peace, patience, kindness, goodness, faithfulness, gentleness, and self-control (Galatians 5:22-23)…these are the foundations you want.

HOW DOES THIS WORK?

When you have a poor self-image, you don't value yourself. You are always looking in a mirror for a reflection of something else you wish you had. I hope you take it seriously to recite that paragraph from Lesson One! You will notice a difference in the way you see yourself plus the love the Lord has for you after repeating that a few times a day. Day after day, after day, after day!

Since we are addressing the concept that *you are worth **waiting** for*, you may be wondering how to prepare yourself during the wait. Good question. Everybody wants to know what to do "in the meantime." Remember, sex in its rightful context of marriage is so fulfilling, so special, holds no guilt, and, in God's heart, is in your best interest! During the wait, you may need to work on some personal areas of your own. Let me encourage you to consider a few areas that may need some real help and attention.

SELF-RESPECT

Self-respect in Webster's dictionary means "a proper regard for one's own person, character, or reputation." The Bible says it this way: "A good name is to be more desired than great riches." (Proverbs 22:1) "Good name" refers to your reputation.

Something that is quite noticeable in our culture today is the lack of self-respect so many teenage girls have for themselves. Low self-esteem brings about low self-respect; so many times, you allow yourself to be treated with far less respect than you deserve.

You control how people treat you by what you think of yourself. If you have no regard for your body—or if you just go with the flow of what everyone else is saying and doing—you will find out very quickly how it will damage your heart. Instead of experiencing the exciting freedom and purity of heart and mind found in doing things God's way, a girl who shows no respect for herself will soon feel weary of the journey and of being manipulated by the world's standards.

CHARACTER MATTERS

Ladies, you have to know that self-respect and moral character matter! People can trust a person of high morals and standards. They know that person is honest and has integrity. So often through TV and movies and even listening to your peers talk, sex seems so casual and is misused so freely. Because they hold no moral standards, they have no self-discipline or self-respect. Purity turns to impurity and causes less than a satisfying relationship with the opposite sex.

However, when you can stand up with courage displaying God-based morality without budging, you will never be disappointed! In fact, it makes your relationship with boys so freeing when you respect yourself and realize that you are worth waiting for! Don't be fooled by what is going on around you or what others may say, boys will love the fact that you are not just one of many but that you are one of a kind!

IT'S MY STYLE

Let's take today's style of clothing. What you wear tells so much about who you are! You can dress sharp without dressing sexy! Today's styles are provocative, shouting a message of take what you can – use what you want. I have spoken to hundreds of teenage boys who say that they struggle tremendously with their thought life over the way girls dress. It causes them to stumble in their walk with the Lord.

Ladies, as women of God and women of character, this cannot be! You, as the Bible says in 1 Thessalonians 4:6 NASB, are 'defrauding your brother', which means taking advantage of him. In God's heart, this is sin, and it must be changed. When you need to seek attention by dressing sexy or wearing sexy clothing as your ploy, you will get much more than you bargained for.

Do you want a boy to desire you just for your body? That is shallow and does not last. You will always be competing with the next "hot" girl who comes along. The girls "getting" boys this way are a dime a dozen. But not you!! Remember, your worth is far above jewels!

Dressing modestly shows respect and asks for respect. You do not need be covered from head to toe, but realize that the way you dress sends off a loud message! What message are you sending? When you honor yourself as the woman God has created you to be, your message will radiate the freedom, confidence, value, and reflection of a girl who believes in herself, knows she is loved, knows she is worth waiting for, and knows who she is in Christ. That, my young friend, will turn the heads of anyone and everyone who notices you walking into a room!

YOU ARE A TREASURE

Treasure, protect, and respect your sexuality. Even if you have given it away, you can always start over again. (We will address this in length in the last chapter). But realize that not everyone is "doing it". You have a gift to give someone. It is not to be cheapened, thrown away, or given away to the highest bidder; it is to be treasured! When something is worthwhile, it is ALWAYS worth the wait! It's time that you start to believe that you are that treasure!

I challenge you to start demanding respect for yourself. Change the way you are thinking. Change the way you may be allowing people to treat you. Believe that you are valued and of great worth. And then trust that when you like yourself, respect yourself, and have friends around you who are walking the same way, you will enjoy the wait!

SELF-CONTROL

Self-control is not for the weak…it is for the strong! It is possessing power, having good sense, sound mind, self-denial, self-sacrifice. It is a discipline not many want to practice. The message screaming at you so loudly from the mass media is that it is unrealistic to ask you to control your sexual appetite. That it is impossible for you to not let your hormones get the best of you! That it is unrealistic to remain a virgin until you marry. What a deadly trap that assumption is to many of you! The Word of God completely begs to differ! The Lord God is not a kill-joy. He is not out to rob you of something. He is out to bless you and give you something of great value and price!

In His extravagant love for you, God has designed the most beautiful way to express intimate love between a man and a woman. And that treasured gift was meant for the marriage bed only. Before sin's pollution, when everything was perfect, sexual pleasure was a treasured part of the creation of man and woman, and God Himself proclaimed it to be very good in the first chapters of Genesis! To be a slave to that pleasure outside of marriage is the world's view of sex. This view defiles sex, making it impure, selfish, and indulgent. It causes you to be a slave to your desires and not a master of them. Therefore, you lose control.

Despite what the culture says, self-control—not self-indulgence—frees you from a broken heart, shattered emotions, deadly diseases, and spiritual detachment. Unfortunately, many Christian teens have

> Self-control—not self-indulgence—frees you from a broken heart.

been deceived and bought the lie that they don't need to control their desires for sex but to indulge them. You are told, "You're just being a kid", or "Who cares, it's no big deal", or "What's wrong with you? It's a natural thing, what are you waiting for?"

IT TAKES COURAGE TO MAKE A STAND

It takes courage to stand up and **choose** abstinence. Self-control is a commitment to yourself, your future husband, and to God that you will not satisfy your desire for sexual activity until the proper time, which, as we have spoken throughout this study, is the marriage bed.

If you want your marriage bed to be the blessed, fulfilling, fun way God intended it to be, then you must understand what the word intimacy means. Intimacy is knowing someone very deeply. It is total life-sharing. It is the joy of knowing someone fully and being known by someone fully without the fear of rejection.

What you are being fed in our culture is instant gratification (just the physical) over intimacy and purity of heart. Remember, we said sex isn't just physical; it's emotional, mental, social, and spiritual. When you engage in sex outside of marriage (and that includes oral sex), with every partner you are with, you lower the significance of sex with your future spouse.

Intimacy and getting to know someone so fully can only come with time, commitment, faithfulness, great friendship, respect and unconditional love through the marriage bed.

The Word of God specifies that when a man and woman come together in a sexual relationship, "the two will become one flesh." (Genesis 2:24) You become one with that person not just physically but emotionally, mentally, and spiritually.

I have watched many students have a very hard time breaking up with their boyfriend and not understanding why. Or they would always seem to run back to that person. Why? Could it simply be because they felt the bond of being one with each other?

Is what everyone is encouraging you to do for temporary pleasure worth what you will lose in the long run?

"No temptation has seized you except what is common to man. And God is faithful; He will not let you be tempted beyond what you can bear. But when you are tempted, he will also provide a way out so that you can stand up under it."
—1 Corinthians 10:13

You are asked by the world to bury and ignore your heart, your emotions, your self-esteem, your self-worth, your self-image and, most importantly, your freedom. This is completely opposite of the plan God has given you!

God wants your sexual experience to be the best He intended it to be! It was His idea from the start. He knows the reasons why He placed the boundaries. They were completely and lovingly for your good and your ultimate pleasure! To lose sight of that is to lose out on the greatest gift and the ultimate, intimate relationship that a man and woman can have together here on earth!

Remember, it was God who noticed that Adam was alone: "It is not good for man to be alone, **I WILL** make a helpmate suitable for him." (Genesis 2:18) Adam didn't ask, God had noticed! He wanted man and woman to walk together, share their hearts, share sexual pleasure, have children, enjoy each other's companionship, comfort each other through the ups and downs of life, and love the Lord their God with all their heart, mind, soul and strength! He calls it very good, and He knows one of the best ways it can be obtained is through self-control!

PRACTICE SELF-CONTROL

Think about athletes who are serious about excelling in their chosen sport. They are disciplined and self-controlled when they want to compete and excel at a level that will give them their greatest victory, gratification and satisfaction.

They can't sit around eating fast food and chocolate, drinking colas, barely practicing, and then expect to compete at the level they want! They must practice self-control, self-denial, and self-sacrifice!

The same is true when you are practicing self-control with relationships. You can't sit around watching TV, movies and listening to music that have so much sexual content in them and then expect to keep yourself pure in thought and action. It simply doesn't work that way. As you are looking to stay pure in a reckless world, you **must** practice self-control, self-denial and self-sacrifice!

"Everyone who competes in the games goes into strict training. They do it to get a crown that will not last; but we do it to get a crown that will last forever. Therefore I do not run like

a man running aimlessly; I do not fight like a man beating the air. No, I beat my body and make it my slave so that after I have preached to others, I myself will not be disqualified for the prize." —1 Corinthians 9:25-27

LOOK ONE MORE TIME!

The fact is that you are worth waiting for! Self-control, self-respect, and self-image are all attainable through the love of God and the help of good friends and family.

God is not holding anything back from you. He is holding something great for you! He values you. You are a worthy vessel of honor to Him. That is why it breaks His heart to see so many of His daughters falling prey to the world's system of sex and relationships.

The greatest thing you could possibly do right now is make yourself ready for all He has planned for you. Some of you may have to make some hard decisions to make a 180-degree turn to get back on track. That's ok, that's what God's love, mercy, and forgiveness are all about. He loves you so! And some of you are already on the right track.

Either way, you are all to grow as women of God: confident in who you are as a single person, able to be self-controlled in your relationships, knowing that your worth is far above jewels. Then, at the appointed and proper time in God's detailed plan for your life, you will receive the man of God that He has chosen for you.

Receiving God's choice for a husband is a gift. In preparing yourself now, have you been treating that gift as you should? When a gift is of great price, it is handled differently than any other gift. May this pursuit you are on as you wait for God's best make you realize the priceless gift that sex is in the marriage bed. And may you recognize more and more the difference between the holy pleasure God has ordained for you and the counterfeit that the world offers through sex outside of marriage.

Journal Entry:

Please go to Appendix A in the back of the book, Day Two, to complete all questions and journal entries that will help you to think and make the necessary changes in this area of sexual purity.

Assigned Homework:

Write your answers to the following questions in your journal in Appendix A.

1. Write a few sentences about the value of having one true friend.

2. Why is "friends with benefits" so rampant among teens?

3. What is your opinion on the following..."how far is too far" to go physically with a boy?

A PERSONAL TESTIMONY...
BETTER THAN FAIRYTALES

"To bestow on them a crown
of beauty instead of ashes..."
—Isaiah 61:3

I was 13 when my mother took me out to dinner to present me with my promise ring, a ring signifying my promise to the Lord that I would keep myself pure until marriage. When I was 14 I gave my virginity to my boyfriend. He had been begging me for months and I thought I'd lose him. Afterwards, I remember thinking, "I guess that wasn't that big of a deal." The more it happened, the less I thought about it. Until, that is, the day my father caught me asleep in my bedroom with my boyfriend. I will never forget the look on my dad's face when I had to give him my ring back. It was only the second time in my life I had ever seen him cry. The hurt I caused my dad haunted me for years. It wasn't much longer after that that I found out my boyfriend had cheated on me. My world fell apart around me. The hurt in my heart was so great I thought I'd never heal. And it would be many years before I felt whole again.

When I was 16 I accepted Christ into my life for the first time. I also started dating the most godly guy I'd ever met. He taught me how to love Jesus; I taught him how to push the limits of impurity. My past sin was coming back to haunt me and now I was trying to take someone else down with me. Ultimately I pushed this amazing guy away.

Shortly after that I started dating the hot, "bad boy" from school. He'd be the guy I'd give myself to in every way. In my mind he was it; he loved me and we were destined to live happily ever after. Until we broke up with each other...(notice my pattern). Yet I couldn't leg go of this guy. I guess God wasn't kidding when He said, "and two shall become one..." I truly felt like part of me was missing without him. When he finally found someone else, I was reminded again of the pain I felt back when I was 14 and lost my first "love." This one hurt more. I never thought that would be possible, and it took much longer to heal. I found myself getting attached to any possible guy I could find. I dated a few more guys, giving myself sexually each time, hoping to feel whole all over again.

Unfortunately I was not done with this cycle until I was partying like a careless soul at 21 years old, when I was slipped a pill and raped. I remember thinking that it wasn't any different from the times I had willingly given myself. And that's when it hit me... the beautiful, wonderful, magical, gift God had given to all of us for marriage felt ruined. I had no one to blame but myself, and I didn't know how to make it right. The overwhelming guilt and shame hit me like a train. I didn't know "rock bottom" could be so tortuous. At this point, I had nowhere to look, but up. I finally said, "Enough", and decided to give everything to God, including my "love" life. To my surprise, He took it.

For the next two years I had found myself again and forgiven myself, finally. It didn't come easy and there were days I don't even remember living, but God had restored in me something I thought I would never see again...my self-worth. I realized that I was still precious and worth living for. I began to like myself once again. I meditated on the verse, "that He casts our sins as far as the east is from the west"...(Psalm 103:12). Not that He didn't remember my sins, but that He chose not to remember them. That somehow meant more to me knowing that after everything I had done, He still chose to love me and chose to see me as white as snow. When I finally realized that, I began to love myself once more.

God's grace has overwhelmed me and I've been able to use my life's testimony for the good of others. Somehow, through everything I've done, God has been able to turn shame, guilt, and death into redemption, hope and guidance. I got married at 25 years old to a wonderful man. God is still with me. He continues to renew me and hold me. I know He will never let me go. I am forgiven and free. I know God never intended me to learn things the hard way, but He's been able to use my mistakes for His glory.

Caroline

Chapter 3

It's All About Choices

"Therefore be careful how you walk, not as unwise men, but as wise, making the most of your time, because the days are evil. So then do not be foolish, but understand what the will of the Lord is." —Ephesians5:15-17 NASB

Y ou are in a unique place in life right now where relationships mean a whole lot to you. From now through at least your first four years out of high school, your peers, friends, and guys will be pretty much a top priority to you. You need to be at a place where you choose these friendships and whom you are going to date wisely!

There are so many good things ahead of you regarding relationships, but if you don't have standards, goals, true understanding of what you want, and the truth of God's Word, you will fall for anything.

You absolutely DO NOT want to be naïve and immature in this area at this time in your life. This is not the time to compromise your life just to have friends. Friendships can accomplish a lot for you, and one good friend can make a huge difference in your life. But one bad friend can do the same thing. The Bible says in 1 Corinthians 15:33 NASB that "bad company corrupts good morals." How will you choose?

MAKING CHOICES CAN BE VERY DIFFICULT

Every area we address in this chapter will concern choices that have to be made individually. Some are tough choices where you may need to end a friendship or a relationship with a guy that you know is not God's best for you. There will be choices to make once you set standards and try sticking to them. A choice may come when you see the progressive actions of "how far is too far" and the importance of where you draw the line.

> You are being called upon to have high standards, and that comes with a price!

Whatever the situation may be, all of these choices come with consequences. If you make good choices, you will reap good and positive consequences. If you make bad choices, you will reap bad and negative consequences. The ball is in your court! You are being called upon to have high standards, and that comes with a price!

Please take *seriously* the choices you are making in your life. As you read this chapter and start to make some choices for yourself, I trust that you will let the Lord show you His goals and His strategy for your life at this time. He will show you how to choose wisely if you will only ask Him!

FRIENDSHIPS

As I said in the introduction above, friendships are very important at this time in your life. Many times you'll find yourself going along with the crowd because you want to be a part of a group. Though it is a normal thing to do, often that is not a wise thing to do.

When you are comfortable with who you are, you won't be so caught up in having to be like everyone else. You'll know the true art of being a good friend and having a lot of friends. Remember, you will be known by the kinds of friends you choose. If those you hang around with don't have a good reputation, you can be lumped in with them and have your reputation questioned, even if you don't participate in the things they do. Not wise…it's a choice.

Often, as both teenagers and adults, we can become so needy, so reliant on friends that we become dependent on them for our own sense of self-worth and happiness. If that is you, always waiting for a phone call, e-mail, text, for someone to get back to you, validate you—and you get mad if they don't respond—you have allowed people to fill a space, a void that they aren't capable of filling. This happens so often.

I think we fail to realize we are doing this until we start being offended, feeling insecure and overly sensitive about what everyone else is saying or doing. My friend Christy calls this "relational idolatry." She wisely says, "Relational idolatry is sin...no different than bowing down to the golden calf. Making people our idol doesn't look bad from the outside...it can look loving and encouraging...but when one person is 'worshipped' more than God, you have landed right in the middle of a stronghold that was cleverly disguised by the enemy."

You must look to the Lord for your sense of value, acceptance and self-worth, not people! Doesn't that make an incredible amount of sense to you? I challenge you to truly examine your friendships. Think about where you are with them. Are they healthy? Are they good for you? Are they grounded in the truths of God's Word?

A TRUE FRIEND

I also want to encourage you with a few things that describe what a true friend really is:

> A *true friend* will laugh with you hysterically over things, and cry with you over other things.

> A *true friend* trusts you with confidential information about their lives. They know it will not go anywhere. It really will remain between the two of you.

> A *true friend* would never pressure you or push you into doing something wrong. They will always have your best interest at heart.

> A *true friend* is loyal to you. Not talking about you behind your back. You know they will always be there for you.

> A *true friend* holds you accountable in every area of your life. They are not afraid to be in your face if they see you are going in the wrong direction.

> A *true friend* realizes that when there has been an argument between the two of you, you need to forgive and talk it through with each other as soon as possible. The enemy's greatest tool is to cause division between the best of friends. Watch out for this trap!

And most of all, *a true friend* will want the best for you. They will celebrate <u>your</u> blessings without jealously. You become each other's prayer warriors! You get excited when you see the blessings and answers to prayer that the Lord has bestowed upon each of you!

There is nothing greater in the world, no greater treasure than to have friends you can trust and rely on. Choose your friends wisely. They can make or break your future! "A friend loves at all times." —Proverbs 17:17

THE REASONS FOR DATING

Dating is a very involved subject and one that needs a lot of attention. I think that, and I say this from years of working with teens, you shouldn't date until you are 16 years old, and even then you should double date or group date until you are at least 18 years old. As much as that sounds old-fashioned to you, this is the best way to enjoy the company of the opposite sex without all of the pressure, anxiety, and false understanding of relationships that plagues teenagers.

Today's society puts so much pressure on young people to date. From TV to movies to music, they all present the same thing: "You are no one special if you are not going out with someone." If you don't handle this pressure to date in a healthy manner now, it can set a negative precedent for your life. That is why it is so imperative that you don't rush into dating relationships.

It is healthy to have many friendships in high school, including those with the opposite sex. But so many times, if these friendships become dating relationships, they turn possessive and confining. I hate to burst your bubble, but most of the guys you date in high school will not be your mate for life. Putting so much emphasis on that dating relationship can cause so much unnecessary pain. That is why I believe that group dating is so essential when you want to get to know someone.

HOW ARE YOU PREPARED

There are healthy and good reasons to be dating. A few of them are listed below. Read through them, and then we'll talk further!

- To help build friendships with the opposite sex
- For healthy, mature personal and social development
- For choosing a marriage partner
- For having good, clean fun!
- To help encourage the other person's relationship with Jesus Christ

Society and the media have absolutely warped the whole concept of dating. I know that at this time in your life you may not be thinking about dating someone for marriage purposes. But you must understand that your choices for dating now will follow you into your marriage.

Every time I speak in front of a group of teenagers and ask them if they want to get married one day, 99% of the hands raise. So that tells me you want this for your life, but how are you preparing for it.

It's like this: your grades matter. If your grades are incredibly low your freshmen and sophomore years, you may try to pick it up and do better for your junior and senior years. However, this may not be enough and you may not get into the college of your choice. I have seen this happen numerous times with students. Your grades from your freshmen and sophomore years follow you as an upperclassman and eventually into college!

How much more will the way you date follow you into your marriage! It matters what you do now, because YOUR CHOICES FOLLOW YOU! Don't let anyone tell you differently!

> Your choices follow you!

DON'T CHASE! RELAX!

God is wise. He has a plan. You must have high standards, without compromise, and great moral convictions before you ever decide to date.

Believe me, I have watched so many girls make crazy mistakes just because they *had* to have a boyfriend. Boys know when girls are desperate, and it's not very attractive to them.

Remember, it was while Adam was sleeping that Eve arrived. God knows what He is doing even in these young dating years you are going through. I know that you want to enjoy this time, and you should! That's why group dating is so much more fun! You really get to know someone in an atmosphere like that.

Relax and enjoy this season and time of your life. Make good, clean choices for yourself. This means don't embrace the media's idea of dating. Your definition of dating needs to come from the Word. "Don't arouse or awaken love until it pleases" (Song of Solomon 2:7). You will never regret it!

I have something else I want to share in this segment. Proverbs 18:22 NASB says, "He who finds a wife finds a good thing and obtains favor from the Lord." This may sound like searching for a mate. However, the word "find" means "to discover along the way." So relax and enjoy these years. Have fun with your friends and go on mission trips and enjoy your youth group. When the time is right as you are walking through your journey, you will meet him along the way! Don't get desperate about relationships right now! There is too much life ahead of you for that!

FRIENDS WITH BENEFITS

One sensitive subject that I must address—and that plagues teenagers today—is the concept and choice of "friends with benefits." Friends with benefits are two friends of the opposite sex who are having sexual relationships, mostly oral sex, with each other with no commitment and, supposedly, no emotional attachment. This is a twisted lie!

> Sex with no emotional attachment? That is NOT truth!

This is dumbfounding to me! This makes you cheap! I'm sorry if that sounds harsh but it's the truth! I want to know who in the world decided that this was an acceptable form of relationship with a friend of the opposite sex! Sex with no emotional attachment? HOLD ON! That is NOT truth! That might be what you think is happening... BUT you are actually joining yourself with someone emotionally, physically and spiritually! And unless your heart is hard, there is NO WAY you are not affected by this! It is an intimate sexual act.

You wouldn't believe how many girls are caught in this. You could easily be one of them. Because God made sex to be such an awesome and intimate act between a husband and wife—a commitment of the hearts, the spirits, and the emotions—it would be pretty foolish to think that this kind of casual sex won't affect you!

You can push those emotions away, but they won't be pushed down for long. You will have to deal with them!

THINK AGAIN

It is unwise and immature for you to think that this kind of lifestyle is helpful to you. I have had numerous girls crying to me because they lost a great guy friend when they became involved in "friends with benefits" and now the guy no longer wants anything to do with them. PLEASE understand that this is such a deterioration of not only you as a young lady, but of your self-worth, your self-image, your peace of mind, your future marriage bed, and definitely your relationship with the Lord.

To bring sex in any form into a friendship with a boy not only ruins that friendship, but it degrades, dishonors, and disregards both people involved and completely severs the trust and confidence that a friendship is suppose to give.

If you need to talk to someone, please find a Christian counselor, a teacher/mentor/Youth Pastor's wife you can confide in and get yourself free and clean from not only the sin of this but of the mindset!

You are worth waiting for. And YOUR choices will follow you! Dating is supposed to be fun! If you choose to date God's way, you will enjoy yourself! You will reap every good benefit that comes with getting to know someone of the opposite sex. You are challenged in a day and age where ANYTHING and EVERYTHING goes. You MUST think outside of that box, and enjoy the journey the Lord has mapped out for you. This calls for great wisdom. Choose wisely!

SET STANDARDS AND GOALS FOR DATING

It is important to do what is right instead of what is popular. <u>This should matter to you.</u>

What is a standard and why is it important?

A standard means to take a strong and aggressively-held position on a matter...to put together boundaries that you will not cross or break so that you can keep your walk pure before the Lord, yourself, your family, and friends. Setting a standard, therefore, means you take the time to write out responsible actions you will allow/not allow in a dating situation.

You *must* have the boundaries set and the line drawn from biblical truths long **before** you go out on a date! We discussed these previously, but one scripture in particular is Song of Solomon 2:7: *"Daughters of Jerusalem I urge you, do not arouse or awaken love until it pleases."* This term "daughters" refers to you girls.

Why is it important to have standards?

You want the guy to know where you stand regarding what you will allow in the relationship.

When you haven't thought about standards/boundaries before you go out on a date, you will open yourself up to so many compromising situations it will make your head spin. You will have to make decisions at times in the spur of the moment. That's why if you already have quality goals, boundaries and standards ahead of time, you will be better equipped to make wise and responsible decisions on matters that you were not expecting or able to handle.

Below are a few standards in several categories. Hopefully this will help you understand.

Physically

What <u>you</u> allow to happen will be the line that is drawn. Some boys will freely take what you are willing to give physically. You MUST have these standards firmly set if you don't want to fall to sexual sin. Answer these questions honestly for yourself.

- What is the meaning of a kiss? What about kissing on the first date?
- What is your response going to be to roaming hands?
- What will your response be to a request for oral sex?

Accountability

It is so good to have someone, preferably a mentor or Youth Pastor's wife, that you can trust and who will hold you to the boundaries and standards you set. Being accountable to someone keeps you honest in your dating relationships and honest with yourself and the Lord.

> Being accountable to someone keeps you honest.

- Discuss your standards with your date up front on the **first** date. So there are no questions about where you stand.

- Avoid being alone as a couple.

- Be accountable to someone else (a friend or mentor).

Spiritually

It is so important that the Lord is number one in all of your life, particularly in the area of male/female relationships.

You must understand that His heart's desire for you is to love Him and others and to be loved by Him and others in return. Then you can have a blast in dating because you will be so free in knowing that you belong to Him and that He wants the best for you! You would not feel the pressure to fall into the culture's way of dating, but you would be accountable to the One who started all this from the beginning. This makes for a very healthy and fun dating experience!

- Date only Christians who have the same convictions as you.

- Pray together before the date asking the Lord to keep your hearts pure and your relationship with Him front and center.

- Ask God for help in choosing wisely whom you will date.

Media

The cultural media—and this includes so many movie stars—are so reckless with relationships. They have no boundaries and, therefore, set no boundaries. If you live your life by their way of thinking, and their promotion of sex, you will fall for things you never thought you would.

If you follow the media's standards, you will lose such a sense of moral right and wrong that your heart will be far removed from the heart of God. You will be shocked at how fast this will happen if you believe the media over the integrity of God's Word.

- Don't put yourself in front of a movie video together at home in his or your game room lying on the couch; it leads to compromising situations very quickly.

- Remember, people in movies and TV aren't really in love or having a relationship. All you are watching are two people acting out fantasy. You have to be careful that any arousal you may feel while watching this with the opposite sex, may lead you both down a path you never intended to fall into.

- The media is out for ratings and to make a lot of money! They are very aware that sex sells! Don't fall into the greed and lust of their pleasure.

Dress/Reputation

"A good name is to be more desired than great riches."
—Proverbs 22:1

Your reputation will follow you, good or bad, and people will know you by the impression you have left when you walk into a room and out again. The friends you keep, and how you dress, talk, and treat others will build your reputation.

- Dress appropriately, meaning stylish yet modest, at all times, around your date and others!

- You can dress sharp without dressing sexy.

- Your reputation, good or bad, will follow you! You have a responsibility in this!

You want to be known as a woman of great character, integrity and good moral judgment. These attributes can only be attained by wise choices, strong boundaries, and a solid walk with the God of the universe.

You MUST have standards and boundaries written out for yourself and thought through LONG before you go out on a date! Make that list **TODAY**!

HOW FAR IS TOO FAR?

"It is God's will that you should be sanctified: that you should avoid sexual immorality; that each of you should learn to

control his own body in a way that is holy and honorable, not in passionate lust like the heathen, who do not know God; and that in this matter no one should wrong his brother or take advantage of him. The Lord will punish men for all such sins, as we have already told you and warned you. For God did not call us to be impure, but to live a holy life. Therefore, (consequently), he who rejects this instruction does not reject man but God, who gives you His Holy Spirit."
—1 Thessalonians 4:3-8 NASB

Obviously, this is a very hot topic. Everywhere I have gone to speak, this is the number one question I am asked: *How far is too far?*

It has always been curious to me why teenagers always push things to the edge; they want to see how close they can go to something before it is called sin. The Bible calls that foolish living. Living that kind of lifestyle will have its downfalls sooner or later. It will bite you back.

ONE FIRST TIME

There is only **one first time** in having sex. It should never be a game to you or a haphazard decision of "who can I give myself to first." A serious and precious gift should only be given to one person.

> There is only one first time in having sex.

The question really shouldn't be, "How far is too far?" The appropriate question is, "How can I get to know this person in a better way personally, and how can we build our relationship together in Christ and in serving others?"

You have a lifetime with your married partner to fulfill the sexual desires that God has placed within each of you. To push arousal to a place of wondering when to stop defies the very purpose of what God intended from the beginning.

Many teenage girls have come to talk to me over the years, mostly Christian teenage girls. After having a sexual relationship with their boyfriend, they all had the same cry of the heart: "I wish I never would have done it." The number-one regret mentioned by every girl was losing their virginity. I don't know of one person who has said to me, "I'm glad I lost my virginity before I got married." Not one! This should speak volumes to all of you!

Do not be so concerned about how far is too far, rather be concerned with how you can be wise in a reckless world, who you are becoming in Christ and what you want to give to your husband in the future.

> *"He who trusts in himself is a fool, but he who walks in wisdom is kept safe."*   —Proverbs 28:26

LOOK DEEPER

Let's see if we can get you to understand a little more about this subject.

When something no longer satisfies, we always want more. That's how most people get addicted to drugs, alcohol, and pornography. Regarding sex, there is a progressive action that takes place as well. When you do one thing for a certain amount of time, it eventually won't be enough; you will want more. The chart below will show you what I mean:

> Holding hands → hugging → kissing → prolonged kissing → touching private areas with clothing on → heavy touching of private areas with some clothes off → sexual intercourse

Look at the progressive action that is taking place. Holding hands is the start of a physical relationship, and then the progression begins.

The problem with many teenagers today is that they seem to go from holding hands to oral sex in just a few dates. Somehow, they seem to think that this is ok and that the line is drawn somewhere with that. I did not put oral sex on this chart because so many teens are confused by that sexual act. It will be explained more in Chapter 5.

I'd like to add here that when you jump from holding hands to a sexual act so quickly, it is only lust. You can try to justify it…thinking that it's love in just a few dates, but in actuality it is just lust. You miss out on a friendship being built between the two of you. You are pushing for something that has dire consequences and trying to justify it as ok. In the process, you are ruining what could have been a great relationship with someone.

WAYS TO THINK ABOUT

One way to know that you have gone "too far" is if you create in someone a desire that you cannot fulfill and still be pleasing to God.

You have to understand that if a man arouses a woman with a desire to have sex, he is defrauding her (in other words, taking advantage of her, as we just read in the opening scripture of this segment). He has violated her because he is not her husband, and he cannot satisfy those desires within the boundaries God has set up. *If you both want to keep your relationship pure and within God's plan, you need to talk to each other.* You do not want to draw out physical desires that will cause the other person to stumble.

You need to realize that guys are aroused by sight, and girls are aroused by touch. Once your hormones have been aroused, you begin to limit your freedom to make wise and clear choices. This is why it is imperative to have already made up your heart and mind about your standards and where the line is drawn—and stick with it!

You have also gone too far when you cannot make sensible and responsible decisions and act on them immediately. Making out prepares the body for sexual intercourse and causes your feelings and emotions to overpower your mind and cloud your decisions.

These are just a few ways to help you recognize the buttons you have pushed that can easily lead you over the edge in this area. Because sex is such a powerful desire, it is ignorant to think that you can go so far and then stop.

Your flesh doesn't know or care that you are only 15 or so, or that you want to live a righteous life. All the flesh knows is that it wants to be fed, so however you feed it, it will always want, and sometimes demand, more.

DRAW THE LINE

In drawing the line on how far is too far, the line is to be drawn right after the kiss, a goodnight kiss, and *no further.* Again, one thing leads to another. When you can't righteously satisfy the physical desires building up in that boy you are with, you are headed down a slippery slope to fornication.

As I said above, you have a lifetime with your married partner to enjoy the pleasures of intimacy. Outside of marriage, you will only cheapen it and cause it to be of no value.

> *"'Everything is permissible for me' – but not everything is beneficial. 'Everything is permissible for me' – but I will not be mastered by anything. The body is not meant for sexual immorality, but for the Lord, and the Lord for the body. Do you not know that your body is a temple of the Holy Spirit, who is in you, whom you have received from God? You are not your own; you were bought at a price. Therefore honor God with your body."*   —1 Corinthians 6:12-13, 19, 20

LOOK ONE MORE TIME!

So, in wrapping up this segment, there is a lot to think about and many, many choices to make! You want to be a young woman who is wise, who can make wise decisions long before you are placed in a compromising situation. You need to face up to what you know in your heart to be true. You are at war! The world and the enemy of your soul are out to destroy your mind, your body, and your relationships. You want wisdom beyond your years so that you can be victorious in this great battle for your heart.

I keep saying this, but it bears repeating. **Your worth is far above jewels!** Your worth, your price, is far above rubies. Rubies aren't just thrown around on the ground; they are hard to come by. You will never regret doing the wise and right thing!

Put yourself above the pack. Decide to be the fish that swims in the opposite direction from the tide. You can choose the wide road, which many are on. Or you can choose the narrow road where only a few are called. The choice is up to you! CHOOSE WISELY!

> *"Enter by the narrow gate; for the gate is wide, and the way is broad that leads to destruction, and many are those who enter by it. For the gate is small, and the way is narrow that leads to life and few are those who find it."*
> —Matthew 7:13-14 NASB

Journal Entry:

Please go to Appendix A in the back of the book, Day Three, to complete all questions and journal entries that will help you to think and make the necessary changes in this area of sexual purity.

Assigned Homework:

Write your answer to the following question in your journal in Appendix A.

1. What part does TV, movies, music video's, and music play in your life and the lives of teenagers around you? What impact has it made?

2. Create a collage of ads/pictures/sayings in magazines, internet, etc. that promotes sexual promiscuity. (this activity is for a classroom setting)

A PERSONAL TESTIMONY...
BETTER THAN FAIRYTALES

"You did not choose Me, but I chose you..."
—John 15:16

I grew up in a Christian home with parents who loved me very much. I was taught what the Bible says about purity and abstinence and decided at a young age that I was gong to keep myself pure for both God and my future husband. However, when I switched schools in 9th grade my desire for popularity and acceptance took me down a path that led to compromise and loneliness.

I wish I could say I was dumb and naïve and didn't know better, but I did and that is what made it worse. I chose to hang out with girls who did not have the same standards as me. I guess at first I thought I was superwoman and their lack of similar values wouldn't rub off on me. Ultimately, I was the one that changed not them. This change didn't happen all at once...it was a slow fade.

My life went from desiring to be a missionary and serving God with my life, to doing everything I could to get noticed and asked out. I changed the way I dressed, the way I acted and my relationship with my parents. I started drinking, smoking and sneaking out with guys. I thought I was invincible and put myself into several very bad situations. My view was as long as I didn't have sex with guys, then I was still remaining pure. Maybe in the world's eyes that was true but definitely not in God's. I remember wanting to feel accepted so much that I would just mess around at parties with guys at random that I didn't even care about. The next day it didn't make me feel any more popular or cool, just used and disappointed in myself.

During that time, I was playing my expected "role" in my youth group and my Christian school. Most people did not even know the double life I was living, but I knew. I was reminded of it every night when I would cry myself to sleep asking God to forgive me for what I had just done. Broken, I recommitted my life to the Lord more times than I could count...but I would just slip right back into it the following weekend when I was invited to another party.

The Lord was always at work in my life. He gifted me athletically so that I could excel in sports. In His wisdom, sports became the avenue through which He broke through my selfishness and sin. Because of the effort and care of a Godly woman's influence, I was challenged to live this pure and holy life that God had set out for me. She was a teacher, coach, a mentor and a friend. For her it was not about winning; it was about guiding me through a process of understanding who God created me to be. Without that personal challenge I might not be the woman I am today.

I ended my ungodly relationships and rededicated my life to the Lord for the last time. Through God's forgiveness and grace I was able to start over. Although some of the scars remain, they remind me of God's unfailing love. After graduating high school and Bible College, God sent me oversees to serve Him in the mission field for a while. And I am grateful that I am still serving Him today.

Now I am a blessed wife, mother of four, and God is using me to mentor others the way it was modeled to me many years before.

Beth

Chapter 4

The Selling of Desire

"Do not conform any longer to the pattern of this world, but be transformed by the renewing of your mind..."
—Romans 12:2

There is a battle going on for your attention, for your heart, and for your life. The world is calling after you and the Kingdom of God is calling after you. They are in complete contrast to each other or they are at war with one another. The one you give the most attention to, the one you allow to speak to you the most, will be the one you follow!

I will probably step on a lot of toes in this section of the study, but I'm not looking to sugar-coat anything. I have no desire to be politically correct, I desire to tell you truth! There is much to say, so let's get started! **Lights...Camera...Action!**

LIGHTS!

The entertainment industry reflects the culture we live in. There is an onslaught of distorted images and ideas of how we are to live our social lives. Daily exposure to this kind of message will affect the way you think and the way you will respond to life decisions.

When we use the term "the world," we are referring to the system of the world—what that system believes, its behaviors, and its way of thinking—that is completely opposed to the Word of God and, of course, to the Kingdom of God.

Please understand, there are two voices crying out for your attention. Once you become de-sensitized to the deception in the world system, the Kingdom of God will seem old-fashioned and non-relevant to you, with all of its moral values simply to be disregarded. Before you even realize it, the world has so completely influenced your heart and disguised the truth of God's Word, that you end up looking like the world even while you are saying that you are still a child of God. It's time we change that. It's time to take back the Kingdom of God in your life.

> It's time to take back the Kingdom of God in your life.

"Do not love the world, nor the things in the world. If anyone loves the world, the love of the Father is not in him. For all that is in the world, the lust of the flesh and the lust of the eyes and the boastful pride of life, is not from the Father, but is from the world. And the world is passing away, and also its lusts; but the one who does the will of God abides forever."
—1 John 2:15-17

The media (which consists of TV, movies, internet, music, e-mail, facebook, myspace, youtube, texting, twitter, books, magazines, advertising commercials, cable news, and newspapers) is today's means of communicating with others. If you can't or don't recognize the counterfeit that lies in a lot of these, you will fall desperately into the world's system.

What much of the media is doing today is giving you false values, a false sense of love, and a false sense of security. Ladies, don't be fooled. The majority of what you see and hear is a direct attack on you as a young woman.

What Are You Believing?

The world's media knows how impressionable young girls are. If they can get you to believe that the only way you can win a guy's heart is to be a size 2 and have a beautiful body, then you are theirs to control. Every magazine you pick up or see at the store checkout line shouts very loudly "You will never get anyone to love you unless you look like this!"

It completely devalues the very person God has created you to be. The advertising industry knows exactly what it is doing. Somewhere, somehow, they have convinced girls/women that they aren't enough. You are devalued because you have none of the outward things that "the world" calls worthy.

This can cause **anorexia and bulimia** in many girls looking to find value in appearance or what society values as "the in look". Many girls fall for this and find themselves in a battle for their very lives. Low self-esteem, poor body image, perfectionism, need for control, loss of a loved one are only a few of the causes of anorexia or bulimia.

The Counterfeit

Please realize that what the world paints is a false sense of security. It is a counterfeit to the real thing. Their idea of the value of a person is only based on the outside appearance! No one can live up to that. If they could, then why do they airbrush every picture on a magazine cover? And why are some of the most beautiful cover-girls on their 3rd marriage? You must understand that outside appearances don't satisfy or last.

> What the world paints is a false sense of security.

"Your beauty should not come from outward adornment, such as braided hair and the wearing of gold jewelry and fine clothes. Instead, it should be that of your inner self, the unfading beauty of a gentle and quiet spirit, which is of great worth in God's sight." —1Peter 3:3-4

If you have a problem with either anorexia or bulimia I urge you to get the help you need. I witnessed girls with this problem as a teacher. What started out to be something they thought they could control, became a monster within. You will need professional help to see you through. Please get the help you personally may need, or a friend may need. No one was ever meant to live in this kind of prison.

If you can only keep a guy because of the way you look, that is a false sense of value concerning love, commitment and relationships as a whole. The media portrays relationships so often as passionate and romantic when in reality they are shallow and self-centered. Many times these relationships are glorified yet they have no standards, no guidelines, no rules, no shame, seemingly no guilt—there is no substance. When they tire of one person, they move on to the next. That is a world view, one that is in complete contrast to the Kingdom of God.

Stop! Get Personal

I am asking you to stop at this point and grab a piece of paper. Be really honest with yourself. What are you basing your life and relationships on? Think about these questions and answer them honestly for yourself (no one is looking!):

- If you are sexually active, why?

- Are you persuaded the majority of the time by relationships you see through movies and TV?

- Do you base your value on your appearance instead of who you are on the inside?

- Would you be willing to sacrifice your Christian walk just to fit in to the world system? Or should I ask, have you sacrificed your Christian walk and are you fitting into the world's system right now?

After you have answered these questions, you may need to make a game plan on how to change your way of thinking. What are you watching and who are you comparing yourself to?

I am not saying that you can't be attractive and always look your best. What I am saying is that your life cannot consist of what the world's value system says is right. Those in the world's system have no intention to honor God in any of their decisions. They do whatever feels good, or seems right to them, being held accountable to no one.

Who Will You Be Giving An Account To?

Think of it in this way: when your life on earth is over, you won't be standing before the world giving an account for your life. You *will* be standing, however, before the King of Kings and Lord of Lords to give an account.

No matter how popular and seemingly free in spirit these celebrities live their lives, they also one day will bow their knee before the only King of Kings and Lord of Lords. The Bible declares that *every* knee will bow and *every* tongue will confess that Jesus is Lord. So this tells us that every celebrity; entertainer; talk-show host; writer, producer, and director of TV, movies and videos; singer; songwriter; and dancer will all one day bow their knee before Jesus. So I ask you again, are you willing to sacrifice your true relationship with the Lord for the world's system?

Look at where you are in your life right now. You are serving one kingdom or another. Which one are you serving? Which one has your undivided attention?

"It is written: 'As surely as I live, says the Lord, every knee will bow before me; every tongue will confess to God.' So then, each of us will give an account of himself to God."
—Romans 14:11-12

Think Like The Kingdom of God

I would like to share the story of one of my former students. I believe this will help you understand that when you think like the Kingdom of God, you will have to make some tough choices at times in your life.

Tammy has been an officer in the United States Navy for over 10 years. Being a female in an environment with so many men, Tammy needed to be very sure of what she wanted in a man she would marry and who she was as a woman of God. She related to me a story that happened to her early in her career.

She was asked out to dinner by a guy she was beginning to date. At dinner that night, she was very upfront with him and told him she wanted him to know that she would not sleep with him at any time in the relationship. That she was saving herself for marriage and wanted him to know right off the bat where she stood with that issue. After a bit of time, he excused himself to go to the restroom and never returned to the table. He left her at the restaurant. She had to call a friend to come and get her. Of course she cried over the

situation and was hurt. But she was not going to compromise her life or her heart to anyone until she made it to the altar.

Tammy is married now with one child and another one on the way! Her decision did not keep her from her heart's desire for marriage and children. She could have very easily gone with the world system, what the world calls normal: sleep with whomever you date. But she chose another Kingdom.

CAMERA!

I'm going to address something that no one likes to talk about at length, but we have to. We have allowed the world system to infiltrate the church. The lust of the flesh, the lust of the eyes, and the pride of life!

We're beginning to see no difference between the world and the church. Teens are just as sexually active in the church as they are in the world. You are taking your cues from another kingdom. And you have been duped. It all sounds good, and the media tries to make it all look good, but you are being seduced by a world disguising itself as freedom.

> You are being seduced by a world disguising itself as freedom.

Seduction: A False Promise

The world system is all about seduction and lust, trying to convince you that your passions are to be indulged rather than controlled. The words *seduction* or *seduce* according to Webster's dictionary means "to persuade to disobedience or disloyalty; to lead astray usually by persuasion or false promises." Seduction is dressed up to be one thing, to flatter you, and then trap you. The seduction I am talking about is the one coming from the world's view of sex outside of marriage.

Do you notice how often you are being seduced when you turn on the TV? How about when you are at the movies? Start paying attention to what you are watching with your eyes: what you see, read, and take in through your eyes will greatly affect your view of the quality of sexual fulfillment.

Look at the romances portrayed on TV and in the movies. Not much friendship or relationship occurs. Within 1-2 days, they are madly in love with each other and involved in a sexual relationship. Teenagers see this and act it out – expecting the same instant gratification. You have just been seduced into thinking it is love when all it has been is lust disguised as love through seduction. The greatest seduction is that the media makes it all look so very enticing!

Look how many soap operas there are on TV. They are no longer just on in the afternoons; there are plenty on in the evenings. They are meant to make women dissatisfied with their boyfriend or husband in hopes that there is a McDreamy somewhere in their path!

Take Notice

If you really take notice, you will also find yourself actually rooting for a divorce so that the woman can be with the other man! Adultery in its finest form! All of this seduction is based on a false promise of forbidden love with no consequences. It's a way of cheapening sex and worse cheapening love.

So often so many TV shows, movies, songs written and sung, are wrapped in the spoils of seduction! Once sex is presented with no boundaries like this, the door is opened to all kinds of perversion. When God tells you to abstain from all of this behavior, it's an act of His love for you. He is not *trapping* you in anyway. He is *protecting* you in every way.

When you lust after things—having an intense desire for something—it begins to rage a war within your soul. The world system says that sex is used to gratify lust and desire. There is no love, no commitment, and no responsibility involved. When you fall to the seduction of the world system, it begins to choke the life of God's truth and His Word right out of you.

The Death Squeeze

Take a minute to imagine a python snake. A python doesn't poison its victims like the rattler or cobra. Instead, the python squeezes the breath out of its victims. What I see happening to so many Christian teens is just like the death squeeze of the python. As you begin to compromise your morals and give in to the world's system of casual sex, the world system, like that python snake, begins to slowly wrap its mindset and behavior around you and choke the very truth of God's Word and nature out of you!

First you are deceived and then slowly but surely you begin dying spiritually and emotionally. I always wondered why so many seniors, after they graduated from Christian high schools, were seduced into the world system within the first three months of their college experience. Something was out to squeeze the breath of truth out of them, and unfortunately it didn't take long to succeed.

The world system is powerful and alluring, but it can only get the upper hand on you if you are not bathed in the truth of God's Kingdom and His Word! Every student I have spoken to that has returned from being persuaded by the world's system has said the same thing, "It cost me more than I thought I would have to pay." Please WAKE UP! The seduction of the world's system is a counterfeit to the very thing you are longing for: true love!

Disloyal

Lust and selfishness are designed to lure you out of the will of God. When you reduce love to lust, it blinds you to the worth of others and the glory of God. It will corrupt your life! It leads you into disobedience and disloyalty!

Remember that part of the definition to seduction is disloyalty. Disloyal to whom or to what? Disloyal to God, yourself, your friends, your family, and the ministry God has planned for you! That's exactly what the enemy is hoping it will do to you so that you won't fulfill the very destiny God has in mind.

Once you fall for this, you end up having no desire to do the things of God in your life. Your worship will stop, your desire for youth group will stop, you will become bored at church, and you will no longer spend time alone with the Lord. So you see, when you stand along side the world's system in the area of immorality, you will lose more of yourself than you ever thought!

ACTION!

It is time to step up!

As you recognize the contrast between the world and the Word, you are going to need to take clear action and make crucial decisions. Not easy but possible. Your future depends on it!

In taking action, you must begin to let go of areas in your life where the world's system has more authority over your life than the Word does. That is always difficult to do, but you will never be able to move on to what God has designed for you unless you let go of what is holding you back.

Work It Out

You are about to go through training! You have to re-train your mind, your way of seeing things, hearing things, thinking things, and saying things! When you start to train **your eyes** toward a pure heart, you will start to notice that what the world offers is cheap. When you start to train **your ears** toward a pure heart, you will start to notice that what the world offers is foolish. When you start to train **your mind** with the Word of God, you will see that much of what the world offers is drenched in lies and deception.

When you go through training, it will require commitment, courage, and tenacity unlike anything you've done before. You will need to turn some things off, stop going to certain places and parties, choose different friends, and get involved in a good youth group. We are talking about re-training years of thinking for some of you. This will take time and commitment to accomplish! But I challenge and encourage you to take the action that is needed to be free from the pollution that the world has blown in your face.

> *"It is for freedom that Christ has set us free. Stand firm, then, and do not let yourselves be burdened again by a yoke of slavery."* —Galatians 5:1

One of the best ways to go through training is with another friend who is looking to walk in the integrity of the Kingdom instead of the world. Then you will be able to walk this out together. Setting goals and getting your eyes, ears and mind thinking truth over lies.

What Are The Contrasts?

Below are some examples of the contrast between what the world says and what the Word says.

When you allow lust, selfishness, and seduction to lure you in, you begin to think and act as the world does. The world's view suddenly becomes your view.

- **The world says**, "Live together, marriage is old-fashioned, you don't need to get married."

- **God says**, "Let marriage be held in honor among all and the marriage bed be undefiled..." (Hebrews 13:4 NASB)

- **The world says**, "There is nothing wrong with being a homosexual or a lesbian, or marrying someone of the same sex."

- **God says**, "Therefore God gave them over in the lusts of their hearts to impurity, that their bodies might be dishonored among them. For they exchanged the truth of God for a lie, and worshipped and served the creature rather than the Creator, who is blessed forever. For this reason God gave them over to degrading passions; for their women exchanged the natural function for that which is unnatural, and in the same way also the men abandoned the natural function of the woman and burned in their desire toward one another, men with men committing indecent acts and receiving in the own persons the due penalty of their error." (Romans 1:24-27 NASB)

- **The world says**, "Abortion is ok, it's not a baby yet. Besides it's my right, my body, my choice."

- **God's Word says**, "For you created my inmost being; you knit me together in my mother's womb. I praise You because I am fearfully and wonderfully made; Your works are wonderful, I know that full well. My frame was not hidden from You when I was made in the secret place. When I was woven together in the depths of the earth, Your eyes saw my unformed body. All the days ordained for me were written in Your book before one of them came to be." (Psalm 139:13-17)

- **The world says**, "It's just sex; it's your hormones; you're young, enjoy yourself now; if it feels good, do it; you can't help yourself."

- **God says**, "Do not be deceived, God is not mocked; whatever a man sows, that he shall also reap." (Galatians 6:7 NASB)

Do you see the contrast? Now is the time to take action for not only yourself but for your future husband and kids!

Remember, you are preparing yourself as a woman of God with integrity, character, and a solid understanding of His love for you.

You are worth waiting for, but while you are waiting—you can't have one foot in the world and one foot in God.

This needs to be a clean, clear decision to put both feet in one of those worlds! This is your decision. No one can make it for you. I'm here to give you the tools to live a pure heart, a pure life in this reckless world. You have to *want* to! No one can want this more for you than you do for yourself!

So I pose another question: what has the potential to lure you into a trap? What keeps knocking at your heart's door to lure you away to be disloyal to your Heavenly Father? When you know that answer, your training will begin.

LOOK ONE MORE TIME!

> This is a winnable war!

In wrapping up this segment on the media, I want to encourage you in this battle! The fight for your attention rests on your choices and your will! This is a winnable war!

You can make the choice to turn off the TV, stop going to movies that are sexually enticing, stop listening to the music that draws you into sexual impurity, begin walking away from friends that don't want to go where you are headed, let go of the boyfriend you know is not God's will for you. And the list can go on and on.

God loves you so much. He wants you to have the best that this life has to offer in relationship with the opposite sex. And His best is that you live in the boundaries He has set, not bowing to the views of the talk shows and media.

You have the responsibility to protect yourself from the world's view. Will this be a tough road? Absolutely! Is it an impossible road? Absolutely not!

Remember, you are on the narrow road, but that road leads to life! So I challenge you to take the time and begin to ask the Lord's forgiveness if you have fallen into the traps of the world's view. Ask Him to help you sort through your current way of thinking and make some changes.

You don't want to put this off. God has invested so much in you already. There is too much He wants to do in and through your life at this young age. You have the potential to be a world changer! You can encourage those around you to live pure hearts and pure lives. But you can't do that unless you have grasped these truths for yourself, and really begin to stay pure in a reckless world.

You will have the potential to bring many of your friends and peers along with you. Isn't that what it is all about anyway? Don't ever underestimate how the Lord can use you at this time in your life. As a child of the King, you are the most influential player for your generation! What a privilege! What an honor! A jewel of great price!

Journal Entry:

Please go to Appendix A in the back of the book, Day Four, to complete all questions and journal entries that will help you to think and make the necessary changes in this area of sexual purity.

Assigned Homework:

Write your answer to the following question in your journal in Appendix A.

What do you think you will be missing out on if you walk away from the world system that is pulling you away from the Kingdom of God and truth? After you get your answer, look at it, open your eyes to see any lie you may be believing and take the time to meditate on what the truth really is in the matter.

Read all of Chapter 5 on STD's and Forgiveness

A PERSONAL TESTIMONY...
BETTER THAN FAIRYTALES

"Therefore if any man is in Christ, he is a new creature;
the old things passed away; behold, new things have come."
—2 Corinthians 5:17 NASB

I'm not sure exactly when the change began...I was raised in a Christian home and a Christian school all of my life. I was a good kid, always at the top of my class academically, popular with my peers, a member of the cheerleading squad, student council, youth group, and missions team. My desire was to do the right thing and make my family proud of me. My dad left us when I was 2 years old, and my relationship with him was a roller coaster at best throughout my childhood, but I refused to use that as an excuse not to reach for God's best for me.

In junior high, like most kids, I became increasingly concerned with how others perceived me. I began judging my looks, clothes, friends, behavior-essentially my worth- based on the perception of those around me. Leading into high school, I was in the popular crowd, still at the top of my class, seeming to have everything going for me. And that's when "the pursuit" began.

He was not particularly good looking, but he had what I'll call "the 'it' factor." Captain of the basketball team and when he spoke other's listened. I wasn't interested, but denial didn't faze him, and he was persistent...and subtle. Our relationship started as a friendship in 8th grade. Soon, our phone calls became 4 hour sessions of soul searching. He always knew how to make me laugh, how to make me feel better, how to make me feel special. This relationship continued into high school, even as both of us pursued other relationships. But he was always there for me...with a wink, a note, a look. He "knew" me, he "understood" me , and I knew he was attracted to me.

Once my junior year approached, my relationship with my dad was at an all-time low, and I became especially vulnerable in regards to my self-confidence and self-worth. And he was there. One night after a basketball game, he kissed me, and everything changed. Our relationship started on the "down low" as we called it, which in reality meant it was secret...and a very dangerous place to be. Somehow, the secrecy of the situation made it even easier to slowly give my heart away. It became almost addictive...I needed his words to lift me, to comfort me, to excite me and to get me through the day.

Our relationship started to become more physical. With each step, my adamancy of where I drew the line diminished little by little, but I knew better than to cross "the line." But it was exhilarating, it was exciting, it made me feel alive and worthwhile, and I wasn't going to let it go. So I became more deceptive to my family and friends. We met up as often as we could, and the lines continued to become more clouded. I was partially in denial of what was happening since this was my first physical relationship, but when it happened, I knew. I was ashamed and disgusted with myself. I looked in the mirror, and I didn't even recognize who I had become. When did I become this person? How did I allow it to go this far? The enemy of my soul had subtly broken down my defenses and robbed me of all I believed in. But I needed this guy now more than ever. I was lying to all my friends and family and had distanced myself from all who loved me. He was the only one I could talk to, and now I was the one in pursuit. He strung me along, but now he was the one with the power. He began dating someone else and seeing me on the side, claiming that he loved me, and I ALLOWED it to happen. It was repulsive, and I can't explain why I was so stupid, but I was blinded by the need to have someone care for me and to make me feel special...what I perceived as love was a cheap imitation.

By the grace of God, my mother figured out what was going on, and my whole world was turned upside down. I wept every day and I couldn't even talk to my family or friends. I despised my mother for ruining my social life, but in my heart, I despised myself for ruining my life. Though I had completely turned my back on the Lord, He still had His hand upon my life. I was accepted to a prestigious and very expensive University with a jaw-dropping scholarship. As soon as I delivered my Valedictorian speech, my mother moved me out of the state for the summer to make sure I didn't do anything to jeopardize my well-being or my future. With a broken spirit, I left and never really returned.

My freshman year in college, I met the true love of my life at Campus Crusade for Christ. He was everything I never knew I could hope for. He was "butterflies in your stomach" handsome, popular, involved all over campus, a true gentleman, and a man after God's own heart. He pursued me very respectfully and deliberately, taking time and care to get to know me and protect my heart. He kissed my cheek after our first date and waited to kiss me until we had dated several months, praying for God's leading in our relationship. From the beginning, he was open with me about his intentions, protective of my heart and reputation, and careful not to cross lines that shouldn't be crossed before marriage. I had experienced the pain of love's cheap imitation hidden in the darkness; now I felt my eyes opened to the reality of God's intention all along...love that is true, deep, joyful, and full of possibility. How is it that I could be so blinded to the blessings that God had in store for me that I was willing to risk it all by giving myself away for such a cheap imitation? I was humbled and awakened.

I rededicated my life to Christ and found complete grace and forgiveness. It took a long time for my broken spirit to heal, for my pride to allow me to thank my mom and restore our relationship, and for my heart to be ready to share my past with my future husband. Though he would have had every right to turn from me in search of one more deserving, he held me and wept with me...and then continued to court me in the most loving and romantic way imaginable. Three years later we were married in the presence of all of our family and friends. This was not a relationship of secrecy and shame but of shared joy and promise. I praise God that He chose to redeem and restore me, but the pain and darkness I walked through for those years has left a scar that I can never erase. This pivotal time in my life is forever lost to me because of my foolishness. How I wish I had hidden HIS words in my heart and found my worth in HIM all along.

Pam

Chapter 5

Part One—Not Up for Debate

"Flee sexual immorality. All other sins a man commits are outside his body, but he who sins sexually sins against his own body." —1 Corinthians 6:18

N ow that we've reached this segment, I pray that you are finally convinced that God intended sexual pleasure to be solely for the marriage bed. When God created man and woman, it was never His intention that they would share their bodies with so many other people. That is why there is disease related to sexual promiscuity. Our bodies were never meant to be shared with one person after another.

There is such an epidemic in our culture of STD's all because society insists on doing what is right in their own eyes.

This part-one of chapter five is a little heavy. It is always difficult to expose things that cause heartache and pain. But I don't want to shy away from truth.

SAFE SEX?

If you listen to the media and many people in the educational system, they would have you believe that if you just use a condom, everything will be ok. Why is it that when someone gives you that kind of advice, it is never 100% certain?

Yes, condoms are marketed as a form of birth control. They can protect from some STDs, but none of that protection is certain. The question becomes, why would anyone choose something that is not 100% sure and call it safe or responsible?

The answer is that adult "experts" are so convinced that you couldn't possibly control yourself and choose God's way (it's too old-fashioned and unheard of in this century) that they use safe sex through condoms as a band-aid on this subject. If this is the answer, then why does the statistics show that 1 in 4 teenage girls has an STD? (Center for Disease Control and Prevention 2008) It is a battle that teens are losing!

I have another question for the "experts"..."who has the condom for teenagers hearts and their emotions"? (we'll get to that in a minute!)

I did much of my research through the Center for Disease Control (CDC). The CDC recommends using a condom while engaging in sex outside of marriage. However, in _every_ case when describing each STD, they have determined that the greatest protection against any sexual disease is abstinence or having only one partner!

Now, if they, as a national health program, know what will keep you the safest, why isn't that message heard loud and clear everywhere else? Abstinence is not a safe sex option. It's the safe sex answer!

> Abstinence is not a safe sex option. It's the safe sex answer!

Think of it this way also, would you let someone who was drunk get behind the wheel of their car and say to them, "just put on your seatbelt, you'll be safe enough?" You know you would never do that. I'm sure you've heard the slogan that says, "friends don't let friends drive drunk." Then why the double standard regarding sex and condoms? Think about it.

EMOTIONAL SCARS

Emotional scars from sexual activity outside the marriage bed are very rarely spoken of, yet it is the reason so many girls are depressed and overwhelmed within. How can we ignore that most precious place in each of your hearts, acting like it's no big deal, and "I can handle this?" As much as everyone wants you to indulge in sexual activity whenever you want and with whomever you want, no one has the cure for the broken heart. **Except**...*"the Lord is close to the broken-hearted and saves those who are crushed in spirit."* (Psalm 34:18)

> The Lord is close to the brokenhearted and saves those who are crushed in spirit.

Emotional scars and pain can last a long time. It is naïve to think otherwise. I have spoken to hundreds and hundreds of teenage girls who were an emotional wreck because of the heartache they felt from sexual promiscuity. It can no longer be denied or hidden like no one is feeling anything! Your greatest hope of freedom in your heart and emotions is when you allow the Lord to come into those places and touch you with His heart of love, forgiveness and restoration. Let Him in!

A HEARTBEAT AWAY

Teen pregnancy and abortion...both of these situations will change your life forever. I am sure many of you may know someone your age who has had a child out of wedlock or an abortion and you have watched them struggle through both of those situations. I have sat, listened to, cried with and counseled many teenage girls through both. The heartache and tears were always overwhelming as they were dealing with the emotional exhaustion that someone their age never should have been in a position to deal with.

The girls I spoke with always told me that they realized they were in these situations because their real choice started when they decided to sleep with their boyfriends. That was the first choice...and then the choices kept mounting once they found out they were pregnant. It is not an easy road if you are in a teen pregnancy. It not only involves you, your boyfriend and the baby, but both families. God's grace, love, forgiveness and mercy has helped many girls through these overwhelming situations.

If you know of someone who is in this circumstance, please encourage them to seek help through the Crisis Pregnancy Center near them. They will give support, encouragement and great counseling. They will help families make wise choices. The gift of life hangs in the balance with these situations of teen pregnancy and abortion.

AN UNDENIABLY INTIMATE SEXUAL ACT

I must also address the subject of oral sex. Somehow, in some way, someone has convinced your entire generation that oral sex isn't sex. That it's ok because you are still a virgin.

Let me reassure you that *oral sex is an undeniably intimate sexual act*. It is every bit as sexually intimate as intercourse. And a virgin, as Webster's Dictionary states, is a man or woman who hasn't had sexual intercourse, **and also**, one who is free of impurity or stain. So yes, technically you are holding onto your virginity, **but** you are also sexually active and therefore sexually impure.

You cannot be confused with this. As I said in Chapter 3 with friends with benefits, it is a sexual act that is a deterioration of you as a young lady. Your self-worth, self-image, heart, spirit and peace of mind become broken pieces of you scattered everywhere.

Sexual purity is about the whole person! It's about being pure in spirit, soul, and body; purity of heart and emotions, along with the physical and spiritual. It's a cop-out, a way of getting around the idea of sexual purity, by saying "Oh, this doesn't really matter because I'm still a virgin."

> "*Woe to those who call evil good , and good evil; who substitute darkness for light and light for darkness...*"
> —Isaiah 5:20 NASB

Trying to justify it as ok is a false argument before God. He can't condone that; He loves you too much. God is not buying into the cheap lie that has caused so many of His daughters to degrade their bodies, depraving their heart, mind, and spirit. It is a twisted truth, one that does the same damage as intercourse emotionally, spiritually and sometimes physically.

> Sexual purity is all of you, not just pieces of you.

You want to be a woman pure of heart, soul, and mind. Sexual purity is all of you, not just pieces of you.

> "*So I tell you this, and insist on it in the Lord, that you must no longer live as the Gentiles do, in the futility of their thinking...Having lost all sensitivity, they have given themselves*"

over to sensuality so as to indulge in every kind of impurity, with a continual lust for more....But among you there must not be even a hint of sexual immorality, or of any kind of impurity, or of greed, because these are improper for God's holy people....For you were once darkness, but now you are light in the Lord. Live as children of light...."
—Ephesians 4:17, 19, 5:3, 8

So please understand that oral sex is sex and even though the world is screaming at your generation that it is no big deal because it's not really sex, continues to be the lie keeping young people in darkness and their hearts far away from sexual purity. My charge to you is that you remain in the light...no longer living in darkness!

A SILENT EPIDEMIC

Because Sexually Transmitted Diseases can be a silent epidemic, I chose to take the following material directly from the Center of Disease Control Fact Sheets. This information is given to you to give clear understanding of what is going on with your body when disease has taken over.

All of the information from the Center of Disease Control is in Appendix B at the back of the workbook. Please go there now to read all of the facts that you need to adhere to, then come back to this page!

LOOK ONE MORE TIME!

Ladies, after you have read all of the information from the Center of Disease Control, look at how many millions of people suffer with a sexually transmitted disease! I trust that you don't want to be included in this statistic. Therefore, you are in a perfect position to make wise and healthy choices for yourself **now** that will positively affect you, your husband and children later on in life!

You have a marvelous future ahead of you! You are not just living for the now. There is much living to do—and much to enjoy in the marriage relationship that God has ordained for you in the future! But between now and then, you still have a choice to make regarding your relationships. You can choose to do it God's way, or you can choose to do it the world's way. Your choice will result in freedom or captivity.

You will always be challenged with living a sexually pure lifestyle, whether married or single.

Please note that what God has given so freely, within the boundaries He thought were best, has been warped by a society that wants what it wants, whenever it wants it—but no one wants to pay the price for it! You will always be challenged with living a sexually pure lifestyle, whether married or single. And it all comes down to the issues of the heart. Be diligent to protect and guard your heart.

"Watch over your heart with all diligence, for from it flow the springs of life...Let your eyes look directly ahead, and let your gaze be fixed straight in front of you. Watch the path of your feet, and all your ways will be established."

—Proverbs 4:23-26 NASB

A PERSONAL TESTIMONY...
BETTER THAN FAIRYTALES

Delight yourself in the Lord
and He will give you the desires of your heart.
Commit your way to the Lord;
trust in Him and He will do this.
—Psalm 37:4-5

The blessing of what I learned from being single through high school, through college and into my late 20's is a blessing that grew greater with each passing year and some day will become the greatest gift any one man will ever receive.

What I mean is this...to this day I have never dated a guy, never been intimate with a guy, never had sex with a guy, and have never told a guy I love him. For many that may sound like a person who's really missed out in life, but then you should also know this...I have never had a broken heart; never been fearful of getting any disease or being pregnant, never been abused (physically, emotionally or verbally), and I have never known the guilt of regrets.

I have made and kept more close friends in my life than most people will ever have in a life time (girls and guys). I have graduated with a masters degree; traveled to most all the states in the United States, gone to Mexico, Ireland, El Salvador and backpacked for 4 months in Australia and 2 weeks in New Zealand. I have seen and done more than most get to experience in a life time and I've done it all before turning 30.

Please understand me, along with all the good, there have also been a number of tear-filled discussions with the Lord asking Him when it would be my turn. Each time He has gently reminded me to, "be patient." Micah 7:7 says, "but as for me, I watch in hope for the Lord, I wait for God my Savior; my God will hear me." I know that even on the most difficult of days He hears me and He holds me close and I am reminded to give thanks and praise because His word is truth. His promise is great and His love lasts forever! I trust Him.

Sonia

Part Two—God Is There if You Fall

"And straightening up, Jesus said to her, 'Woman, where are they? Did no one condemn you?' And she said, 'No one, Lord.' And Jesus said, 'Neither do I condemn you; go your way. From now on sin no more.'" —John 8:10-11 NASB

In coming to a close in this series, it is very important that you understand the forgiveness of God. So often when we sin, the guilt or condemnation sits so heavily upon us that we feel we can't ever get things right again with God. What we know in our heads about His forgiveness, we can't seem to transfer to our hearts and really receive that forgiveness. So I want to take the time to give you as much ammunition as I can to teach you how to forgive yourself and others.

"He who conceals his sins does not prosper, but whoever confesses and renounces them finds mercy." —Proverbs 28:13

If you have fallen to sexual sin or sexual activity of any kind—and this includes impure thoughts/fantasies that can grow into monsters in your mind in no time—there is forgiveness with God.

Now I'm not talking about the kind of cheap grace where we ask for forgiveness, knowing full well we will be doing it again next weekend. I'm talking about the forgiveness that has repentance all over it!

Repentance is a 180-degree turn to walk away from *everything* that has to do with that situation and let God clean your heart, mind, and spirit over the matter. An alcoholic, as he is getting free from that addiction, does not hang out in bars. He can't, or he'll fall back to it in no time.

You must walk away, no matter how hard it may be.

SEEK HIS FREEDOM

If you are serious with God, and you want the "plans He has for you," then I am sure He would say to you, "Where I am taking you, my daughter, that sin cannot come with us." You must rid yourself of every hindrance that will keep you from the destiny God has for you. God knows your heart. He will move heaven and earth to help you. But you need to make it your desire!

You can be clean again! It is a process, but you wouldn't believe the freedom that can come to you if you begin to speak certain scriptures over your life. We will talk about these scriptures below.

You see, the enemy of your soul wants you to remain in a pit that you can't get out of. He wants you to feel so awful in what you have done that you won't even seek the freedom that you could have. If he can hold you down, then you won't be effective for the Kingdom of God, and that is his goal for you.

The enemy is banking on the fact that when you have sinned in any way, you will stop your communication with God. This prevents you from praying, and then he has his hooks in you, keeping you separated from the One who has your very answer in the palm of His hand.

SPEAK HIS WORD

Here are a few Scriptures that you can write on 3x5 cards and say out loud to yourself:

"If we confess our sins, He is faithful and just and will forgive us our sins and cleanse us from all unrighteousness."
—1 John 1:9

"Create in me a clean heart, O God, and renew a steadfast Spirit within me." —Psalm 51:1 NASB

"Who is a God like you, who pardons sin and forgives the transgression of the remnant of his inheritance? You do not stay angry forever but delight to show mercy. You will again have compassion on us; you will tread our sins underfoot and hurl all our iniquities into the depths of the sea."
—Micah 7:18-19

"But you, O Sovereign Lord, deal well with me for Your name's sake; out of the goodness of Your love, deliver me. For I am poor and needy, and my heart is wounded within me."
—Psalm 109:21-22

"Wash me thoroughly from my iniquity and cleanse me from my sin. Purify me with hyssop and I shall be clean; wash me, and I shall be whiter than snow."　　　—Psalm 51:2, 7

You can be sure that, in time, you will start to feel clean again because you are clean by the work Christ did at Calvary. I am telling you, ladies, there is nothing, *nothing* that is more freeing than a clear, clean sound mind! It gives you peace and confidence, and opens you up to hear the voice of God for yourself! Your whole walk will change. I guarantee it!

GOD RESTORES

The Lord is so good. He is so faithful to restore us back. Think of the story of the woman caught in adultery in John 8:3-11. He didn't yell at her, He didn't ignore her, He didn't make her feel awful about her sin. He didn't condemn her, accuse her, or judge her. He simply, lovingly took

> He is so faithful to restore us back.

her by the hand, lifted her to her feet and forgave her...**but** He gave her instructions after He forgave her, to go and sin no more!

Can you imagine how this woman felt? Scared to death I'm sure, naked in the middle of the street with those who wanted to stone her, were gawking at her, trying to trip Jesus up so that they would have grounds to accuse Him. Yet Jesus, in the same heroic way that a Prince might rescue His bride, chose to challenge those who were accusing her.

Remember, he challenged that whoever among them was without sin should be the one to throw the first stone at her! He chose to publicly rescue the one who was laughed at, gawked at, and accused. Only a Savior does that!! And when He asked her to go and sin no more, it was to let her know this is not how she was to live her life anymore.

She was forgiven. She was to be cherished and treated with dignity, not going around to other married men's beds to find her self-worth or false love.

HE SAYS TO YOU, as He reaches out His hand to lift you back on your feet again, "You Are Forgiven! You are worth far more than this. You are a valued pearl of great price. You are cherished and are to be treated with dignity and respect. Stay out of the grasp of young men's beds, for I have someone who will love you as I do, who will be an extension of my love for you. It is through the marriage bed that you will have this kind of relationship that I desired for my children from the start. All the world offers you outside the marriage bed is a false love, a false way to express that love, and an unworthiness of heart and character that I would never want you to carry as My bride, a true bride of Christ."

NO CONDEMNATION

Condemnation is what students have told me they struggle with the most. After falling to sin of any kind, feelings of guilt and condemnation can be so overwhelming.

Isn't it funny how the enemy is the first to tell you what you are doing is no big deal, but then he is the first to condemn you for it after you have taken the bait!

Condemning thoughts rob a person of forgiveness. They are deceptive thoughts of the enemy. Lies that he wants to use to trap you. Once again the truth says, "There is therefore now, **no condemnation** for those who are in Christ Jesus." (Romans 8:1 NASB)

If you have committed your heart to the Lord, you are in Christ, therefore there is no condemnation. God convicts us of our sin so He can draw us to Himself, but He never condemns us.

When you hear that voice of condemnation, you must know that is *not* the Lord speaking like that to you! Satan is always trying to draw you away from God. You cannot believe the lie, you must recognize it quickly so as not to be drawn in and dragged into a pit!

The Lord looks right through you and is not angry or ashamed of what you have done or who you are. He is calling you to be serious about your change of heart! He wants you to accept His forgiveness, repent, forgive yourself, and trust that what He said, He will do!

God will not forsake a broken spirit or a broken heart…He says in Psalm 34:18 NASB that "He is near to the brokenhearted and saves those who are crushed in spirit." He will cleanse you. You will feel pure again. He is for you and not against you! He isn't mad *at* you, He is mad *about* you! Remember: God convicts—the enemy condemns! YOU ARE FORGIVEN!

SECOND VIRGINITY

God is absolutely the God of the second chance! He gives us endless times to get things right. This phrase, second virginity, has become very popular. It is a commitment that many teens are making who have fallen sexually and are now choosing to abstain until marriage.

> God is absolutely the God of the second chance!

Often when the decision has been made to have sex and then there is so much regret afterward, teens seem to think, "Well I already did it so what's the use, I might as well continue." That is a lie from the enemy and a way to stay in the pit much longer than you ever wanted to.

When you make this commitment to second virginity, you are saying that you have made a clear decision that you will wait until your wedding night before you share yourself intimately with a man. Physically you will not retain what you could only give once, **but** God can *and has* restored thousands of those who chose to abstain after having already participated in sexual activity, making their wedding night brand new!

Remember sex is not just physical, it is emotional, spiritual, and mental—the whole person. The Lord can completely restore all of that back to you and desires to do so. He has honored many of those who have chosen to recommit this area of their lives back to Him.

GOD IS WAITING FOR YOU

God is waiting for you to return! Why not start today! Why not make a commitment to be a pure woman of God. Be determined! You are not going back! That is behind you. You are going on with all the Lord has for you until the perfect one comes along! Choose to be a faithful wife and a pure wife. Make a decision: I will be a holy woman of God. I am not going back. That is my commitment!

Do you need to go to the foot of the cross with all of this? Don't delay; He is so willing to set you free and make you clean again. Give Jesus the chance to make all things new!

"…He does not treat us as our sins deserve or repay us according to our iniquities. For as high as the heavens are above the earth, so great is His love for those who fear Him; as far as the east is from the west, so far has He removed our transgressions from us." —Psalm 103:10-12

FORGIVING OTHERS

Though it is the toughest thing to do when you have been wronged, forgiving others for whatever they may have done is the only way you will remain free in heart and spirit! You want to avoid bitterness, jealousy, being offended all the time, anger, frustration, selfishness, and self-pity at all cost! These are the consequences of not forgiving someone, of holding a grudge because you think they deserve it!

> You hold yourself hostage, a prisoner of your own making.

This will hurt no one but you! You hold yourself in bondage when you don't forgive. You hold yourself hostage, a prisoner of your own making. The other person may be freely doing their thing, but you are churning inside because you have gone over this time and time and time again in your mind, and now all of those feelings have grown into monsters over your thought life! You are not even yourself anymore because now you want to get even or make the other person feel just as bad as they made you feel.

I was angry with someone for 10 years—read that again, 10 years—over a matter that was devastating to me. Who do you think got the worst of that situation, me or them? Me! When I recognized the fact that I had no right to hold someone captive in my heart like that and that vengeance was not mine but God's, I was finally free.

If you have hurt someone, you must take the initiative to go and apologize and make it right with that person. You can say that you forgive a friend, but if you shun that person and remove them from your life, you haven't forgiven them from your heart. You also must forgive the boys who have sinned with you in pre-marital sex.

"For if you forgive men for their transgressions, your heavenly Father will also forgive you. But if you do not forgive men, then your Father will not forgive your transgressions."
—Matthew 6:14-15 NASB

THE POISON OF UNFORGIVENESS

Unforgiveness destroys relationships. It causes marriages to end, friendships to part, siblings to stop talking to one another. It is meant to divide and not unite. It is a dangerous hold against someone.

It is the same thing in forgiving yourself. You may have done things that you haven't told a single soul. You may have been involved in sexual sin, or you may be right now while you are reading this. Maybe you had an abortion and none of your friends know. Or maybe it's something altogether different, but you're thinking that no one will like you anymore if they knew! You have learned to hide things, keeping them in the dark. That can slowly eat away at every fiber of your heart and spirit.

In not forgiving yourself, all you are doing is fueling the fire of the enemy, because he knows he can trick you into believing that you have overplayed your hand and now there is no way that God will forgive all you have done. The enemy will make you hold yourself captive, hiding in bondage as a hostage. It's a slow death grip. And when you choose not to forgive yourself, you are simply saying to God, "Your sacrifice wasn't good enough. Your blood wasn't powerful enough to make me whole again,"

But God says to you, "Come now, let us reason together. Though your sins are as scarlet, they will be as white as snow; though they are red like crimson, they will be like wool."

—Isaiah 1:18 NASB

ACCEPT GOD'S FORGIVENESS

> Let Him lift you back on your feet again!

Let yourself off the hook and accept God's forgiveness! It is time to look up, grab hold of His hands that are reaching to you, and let Him lift you back on your feet again! He never made you to live in the pig pen; He made you for the palace! Forgive yourself! He does—and that's the best place to start!

May this prayer help to restore your soul! Say it out loud to yourself until it gets into your heart!

"Heavenly Father, forgive me for all my sins. Let the power of your blood wash away every sin, guilt and shame from me. Wash away even the memories of them from my mind. For I know they are waging war against my soul. Help and guide me in Your truth and teach me all things that pertain to godliness, purity, and true holiness. Thank you for your mercies that are new every morning. Help me to see myself the way You see me, free and blameless before You! Thank you for washing me and making me whiter than snow! I receive and believe Your love and forgiveness for me. In Jesus Name I pray. Amen."

LOOK ONE MORE TIME!

I pray that this helps you understand the importance of forgiving yourself and trusting the mercy of God and His grace over you! You can start again. The Lord will take your heart and with His compassion fill you again with the cleansing power of His love. He wants you free from everything that has held you captive! There is not one thing you have done that He would turn His back or separate you from His love! That is not the God we serve.

The Lord has promised you in His Word,

"...that neither death, nor life, nor angels, nor principali-
ties, nor things present, nor things to come, nor powers, nor
height, nor depth, now any other created thing, shall be able
to separate us from the love of God, which is in Christ Jesus
our Lord." —Romans 8:38–39 NASB

Make it a point to come to Him in the brokenness of your wound-ed heart, He will take that heart and restore it back to what He want-ed it to be from the start. And you will enjoy a relationship with the Lord like you've never known.

You need to also give this the time that is needed. If you don't feel forgiven right away that doesn't mean that your not. It means that you take it as an opportunity in reading His word for yourself, and memorizing scriptures (which I gave you a few in the above text), getting them deep in your heart. You will begin to sense His forgiving power in no time.

You are loved and you are forgiven. If you were the only one on the earth, He would have died just for you! Wrap your heart in that fact, and enjoy the cleansing power of His love and mercy toward you!

Journal Entry:

Please go to Appendix A in the back of the book, Day Five, to complete all questions and journal entries that will help you to think and make the necessary changes in this area of sexual purity.

Assigned Homework:

Write your answer to the following question in your journal in Appendix A.

Write a letter to the Lord, first asking Him for forgiveness in any area of sexual immorality that you may have been involved with and thanking Him for His cleansing power and love to help you start anew as you continue to mature and grow. Those who are walking strong in this area already, thank Him for that strength and ask Him to continue to give you wisdom and understanding as you also continue to mature and grow. I pray every one of you strengthens your commitment to stay pure. Second, surrender what needs to be placed at His feet, and trust Him to bring all things together in its time. Set boundaries that you are willing to make to yourself and the Lord until you say "I do" at the altar! Give Him this area of your life of love, sex and relationships! He knows what He is doing! Trust Him!

A PERSONAL TESTIMONY...
BETTER THAN FAIRYTALES

And we have come to know and have believed
the love which God has for us.
—1 John 4:16

I was determined to be the only woman in my family who did not have a child out of wedlock. I loved God and tried so hard to please Him. I was 16 years old at a party with a girl I did not know very well. We had some drinks and then she left me there. I wanted to go home. A guy at the party offered to drive me to my house. Only he took me to his house and raped me. I felt as if all that was beautiful and pure in me had been taken away. And I was left with nothing but guilt and shame.

In my shame I ran away from God. I ran from church and I ran from home. I began to sleep with many guys. I did drugs and drank. But the shame never went away it only got worse. I was spiritually dead inside; nothing helped.

By the age of 21 I was a young single mother with nowhere to turn. Desperate for help, I thought about coming back to God. It was amazing. I felt as if God had been anxiously awaiting my return because the second I looked to Him, He wrapped me in His love. It was then that I realized, I do not have to work hard to earn God's love and forgiveness. It is a free gift that He excitedly gives us. I felt so pure again. I found worth and value I never knew I had. I am so overwhelmed with God's amazing love for me that no guilt or condemnation can come near my soul. His love is so amazing and I do not deserve it. He died to love me. The Scripture that has ministered to me the most is from Luke 7:47, "Therefore, I tell you, her many sins have been forgiven – for she loved much...."

After turning to God for help and receiving His love, I found a great church. It was there I met the love of my life. I had never known a love like this before. This man loved me and he absolutely adored my daughter. He helped me to understand God's unconditional love. We have been happily married now for over 10 years. We have 3 children who, by the grace of God, all love and serve Him. This is truly what dreams are made of. All because I had the courage to, one day, fall into the arms of a loving God. I am forever grateful. He is good!

Ehricka

Final Word To The Student!

Congratulations! You have just finished a week-long study on how to stay pure in a reckless world. You did a great job!

I trust that giving you the tools within this workbook and in your class time, will help you to have the confidence you need as you finish out your high school and college years.

The way young girls and women are portrayed in our society is not the heart of God. He wants nothing but for you to be honored, respected, cared for, and protected and for you to know in your heart that your worth is far above jewels! You are a princess in the eyes of your Prince! He wants an abundant life for you!

I know that you are under a lot of pressure from the voices of society that make fun of those who choose abstinence or choose to simply start again. It takes great courage to stand up against the crowd. But you are not alone. This is why I purposely put in here a few testimonies of girls who have gone before you. I hope they give you courage, whether you have fallen or not, to keep moving forward.

God keeps, He rescues, He redeems, He restores, and He makes all things new! The Lord will honor your love life when the right time comes! Trust Him with that! He knows what He is doing!

So now it's up to you! You have a choice to make. It is your choice. No one can make it for you! My greatest prayer for you is that you make a choice to value and respect yourself above the noise of the crowd and say no to sex outside of marriage. Remember, you have a great future ahead of you! And there is an appointed time for everything under the sun!

Thanks for giving me the chance to talk with you so candidly on this subject of purity! May you share the hope with others!

God's richest blessings to you always!

Luanne

Appendix A

DAILY JOURNALS

Journal: Day One

What do you want to receive from this study? What do you want God to show you the most about yourself?

_____

_____

_____

_____

_____

_____

_____

_____

Do you trust God has a good plan for your life? In what ways and how?

_____

_____

_____

_____

_____

_____

_____

_____

Explain your understanding that marriage if a gift from God.

_____

_____

_____

_____

_____

_____

_____

How can you avoid the voice of deception in your mind that tells you to reach out and grab the lie, as Eve did in the Garden, to "see, taste, and eat."

_____

_____

_____

_____

_____

_____

_____

From in class assignment:

Pick two of the five Scriptures from the ones listed in chapter one and write them down. Explain why the verses are significant to you personally.

_____

_____

_____

_____

_____

_____

_____

_____

_____

_____

Homework:

Look through your clothes closet. Write down what signals you are sending to adults, to your peers, and to the opposite sex.

_____

_____

_____

_____

_____

_____

_____

_____

JOURNAL: DAY TWO

When you look in a mirror, how do you view yourself? Do you realize your answer will greatly impact the way you let others treat you?

_____

_____

_____

_____

_____

_____

_____

_____

How are you going to change any negative mindset you may have regarding your self-worth and self-image?

_____

_____

_____

_____

_____

_____

_____

While so many of your peers are living recklessly with relationships, how are you going to be different?

_____

_____

_____

_____

_____

_____

_____

_____

From in class assignment:

What are ways you can show respect for yourself in relationship with a boy?

_____

_____

_____

_____

_____

_____

_____

_____

Self-control not self-indulgence frees you from a broken heart. Explain how.

_____

_____

_____

_____

_____

_____

_____

You are of great value to your Heavenly Father! What does that mean to you?

_____

_____

_____

_____

_____

_____

_____

_____

Homework:

Write a few sentences about the value of having one true friend.

_____

_____

_____

_____

_____

_____

_____

_____

Why is "friends with benefits" so rampant among teens?

_____

_____

_____

_____

_____

_____

_____

What is your opinion on the following…"how far is too far" to go physically with a boy?

_____

_____

_____

_____

_____

_____

_____

JOURNAL: DAY THREE

In choosing your friends wisely, what attributes are you looking for in them?

_____

_____

_____

_____

_____

_____

_____

_____

Why do you think it's easier to go along with the crowd instead of standing up for truth?

_____

_____

_____

_____

_____

_____

_____

Have you ever had to make a tough choice in your life? What was it and how did you handle it?

_____

_____

_____

_____

_____

_____

_____

In the topic of having sex before marriage, what are some of the price tags that come with that choice?

_____

_____

_____

_____

_____

_____

_____

If your choices in life follow you, what is one wise choice you want to make for your life now and why?

_____

_____

_____

_____

_____

_____

_____

From in class assignment:

Choose one of the five standards in the workbook that you feel will help you keep yourself sexually pure and explain why you are choosing that standard.

_____

_____

_____

_____

_____

_____

_____

_____

Homework:

What part does TV, movies, music video's, and music play in your life and the lives of teenagers around you? What impact has it made?

_____

_____

_____

_____

_____

_____

_____

_____

JOURNAL: DAY FOUR

What does it mean to be desensitized?

_____

_____

_____

_____

_____

_____

_____

_____

Between the world system and the Kingdom of God, which one has your undivided attention? To what degree?

_____

_____

_____

_____

_____

_____

_____

_____

If something is a counterfeit, what does that mean and how does that relate to you regarding the media?

_____

_____

_____

_____

_____

_____

_____

The world system is powerful and alluring. Give all the ways it is seducing your generation.

_____

_____

_____

_____

_____

_____

The Kingdom of God is very powerful and truthful. Find 3 Scriptures you can stand on as you battle for your freedom.

_____

_____

_____

_____

_____

_____

_____

For in class assignment:

Write out a list of TV shows, movies and music that are saturated with sexual content. Then give at least 4 ways you can take action for your mind, heart and spirit. Remember, you want to live pure in a reckless world...it will take action on your part!

_____

_____

_____

_____

_____

_____

_____

Homework:

What do you think you will be missing out on if you walk away from the world system that is pulling you away from the Kingdom of

God and truth? After you get your answer, look at it, open your eyes to see any lie you may be believing and take the time to meditate on what the truth really is in the matter.

_____

_____

_____

_____

_____

_____

_____

_____

JOURNAL: DAY FIVE

Do you have a real understanding of the effects of STD's in young people's lives? Does it concern you?

_____

_____

_____

_____

_____

_____

_____

_____

Why do you think the culture is so adamant about the safe sex message?

_____

_____

_____

_____

_____

_____

_____

_____

In choosing abstinence, what 3 things can you apply to your life and stick to them at this time in your life?

_____

_____

_____

_____

_____

_____

_____

_____

Do you have a true grasp of God's forgiveness? Explain.

_____

_____

_____

_____

_____

_____

_____

_____

If you have fallen to sexual sin in any way, give 3 ways you can begin to start anew.

_____

_____

_____

_____

_____

_____

_____

_____

_____

Final assignment:

Write a letter to the Lord, first asking Him for forgiveness in any area of sexual immorality that you may have been involved with and thanking Him for His cleansing power and love to help you start anew as you continue to mature and grow. Those who are walking strong in this area already, thank Him for that strength and ask Him to continue to give you wisdom and understanding as you also continue to mature and grow.

I pray every one of you strengthens your commitment to stay pure. Surrender what needs to be placed at His feet, and trust Him to bring all things together in its time. Set boundaries that you are willing to make to yourself and the Lord until you say "I do" at the altar! Give Him this area of your life of love, sex and relationships! He knows what He is doing! Trust Him!

_____

_____

_____

_____

_____

_____

_____

Appendix B

SEXUALLY TRANSMITTED DISEASES
CAUSES, CONDITIONS, CURES

CENTER FOR DISEASE CONTROL FACT SHEET

CHLAMYDIA

What is Chlamydia?

Chlamydia is the most frequently reported bacterial sexually transmitted disease in the United States. In 2006, 1,030,911 chlamydia infections were reported to the CDC from 50 states. An estimated 2,291,000 U.S. civilians ages 14-39 are infected with chlamydia based on the U.S. National Health and Nutrition Examination Survey.

Chlamydia can be transmitted during vaginal, anal, or oral sex. Chlamydia can also be passed from an infected mother to her baby during vaginal childbirth. Any sexually active person can be infected with chlamydia. The greater the number of sex partners, the greater the risk of infection.

Chlamydia is known as a "silent" disease because about three quarters of infected women and about half of infected men have no symptoms. If untreated, chlamydia infections can progress to serious reproductive and other health problems with both short-term and long-term consequences. Like the disease itself, the damage that chlamydia causes is often "silent." In women, untreated infection can spread into the uterus or fallopian tubes and cause pelvic inflammatory disease (PID). This happens in up to 40 percent of women with untreated chlamydia. PID can cause permanent damage to the fallopian tubes, uterus, and surrounding tissues. The damage can lead to chronic pelvic pain and infertility. Women infected with chlamydia are up to five times more likely to become infected with HIV, if exposed.

Babies who are born to infected mothers can get chlamydial infections in their eyes and respiratory tracts. Chlamydia is a leading cause of early infant pneumonia and pink eye in newborns.

Chlamydia can be easily treated and cured with antibiotics. However, persons with chlamydia should abstain from sexual intercourse until they and their sex partners have completed treatment, otherwise re-infection is possible. Having multiple infections increases a woman's risk of serious reproductive health complications, including infertility.

The surest way to avoid transmission of STDs is to abstain from sexual contact, or to be in a long-term mutually monogamous relationship with a partner who has been tested and is known to be uninfected.

HPV

What is HPV?

Genital human papillomavirus (HPV) is the most common sexually transmitted infection. There are more than 40 HPV types that can infect the genital area of men and women. You cannot see HPV. Most people who become infected with HPV do not even know they have it.

Most people with HPV do not develop symptoms or health problems. But sometimes, certain types of HPV can cause genital warts in men and women. Other HPV types can cause cervical cancer and other less common cancers, such as cancers of the vulva, vagina, anus, and penis. The types of HPV that can cause genital warts are not the same as the types that can cause cancer.

Genital warts usually appear as small bumps or groups of bumps, usually in the genital area. Warts may appear within weeks or months after sexual contact with an infected person. Or, they may not appear at all. If left untreated, genital warts may go away, remain unchanged, or increase in size or number. They will not turn into cancer.

Cervical cancer does not have symptoms until it is quite advanced. For this reason, it is important for woman to get screened regularly for cervical cancer.

Approximately 20 million Americans are currently infected with HPV, and another 6.2 million people become newly infected each year. At least 50% of sexually active men and women acquire genital HPV infection at some point in their lives.

The American Cancer Society estimates that in 2008, 11,070 women will be diagnosed with cervical cancer.

For those who choose to be sexually active, condoms may lower the risk of HPV, if used all the time and in the right way. Condoms may also lower the risk of developing HPV related diseases, such as genital warts and cervical cancer. But HPV can infect areas that are not covered by a condom – so condoms may not fully protect against HPV. So the only sure way to prevent HPV is to avoid all sexual activity.

There is no treatment for the virus itself...visible genital warts can be removed by patient-applied medications, or treated by a health care provider. Some individuals choose to forego treatment to see if the warts will disappear on their own. No one treatment is better than another. Cervical cancer is most easily treatable when it is diagnosed and treated early. But women who get routine Pap testing and follow up as needed can identify problems before cancer develops. Prevention is always better than treatment.

The surest way to avoid transmission of STDs is to abstain from sexual contact, or to be in a long-term mutually monogamous relationship with a partner who has been tested and is known to be uninfected.

GONORRHEA

What is Gonorrhea?

Gonorrhea is a sexually transmitted disease (STD). Gonorrhea is caused by Neisseria gonorrhoeae, a bacterium that can grow and multiply easily in the warm, moist areas of the reproductive tract, including the cervix (opening to the womb), uterus (womb), and fallopian tubes (egg canals) in women, and in the urethra (urine canal) in women and men. The bacterium can also grow in the mouth, throat, eyes, and anus.

Gonorrhea is a very common sexually infectious disease. CDC estimates that more than 700,000 persons in the U.S. get new gonorrheal infections each year. Only about half of these infections are reported to CDC. In 2006, 358,366 cases of gonorrhea were reported.

Gonorrhea is spread through contact with the penis, vagina, mouth or anus. Gonorrhea can also be spread from mother to baby during delivery.

People who have had gonorrhea and received treatment may get infected again if they have sexual contact with a person infected with gonorrhea.

Gonorrhea is known as a "silent" disease because any sexually active person can be infected with gonorrhea. In the United States, the highest reported rates of infection are among sexually active teenagers, young adults, and African Americans.

The initial symptoms and signs in women include a painful or burning sensation when urinating, increased vaginal discharge, or vaginal bleeding between periods. Women with gonorrhea are at risk of developing serious complications from the infection, regardless of the presence or severity of symptoms.

In women, gonorrhea is a common cause of pelvic inflammatory disease (PID). About one million women each year in the United States develop PID. The symptoms may be quite mild or can be very severe and can include abdominal pain and fever. PID can damage the fallopian tubes enough to cause infertility or increase the risk of ectopic pregnancy. Ectopic pregnancy is a life-threatening condition in which a fertilized egg grows outside the uterus, usually in a fallopian tube.

If a pregnant woman has gonorrhea, she may give the infection to her baby as the baby passes through the birth canal during delivery. This can cause blindness, joint infection or a life-threatening blood infection in the baby.

Several antibiotics can successfully cure gonorrhea in adolescents and adults. However, drug-resistant strains of gonorrhea are increasing in many areas of the world, including the United States, and successful treatment of gonorrhea is becoming more difficult. Because many people with gonorrhea also have chlamydia, antibiotics for both infections are usually given together.

The surest way to avoid transmission of STDs is to abstain from sexual intercourse, or to be in a long-term mutually monogamous relationship with a partner who has been tested and is known to be uninfected.

GENITAL HERPES

What is Genital Herpes?

Genital herpes is a sexually transmitted disease (STD) caused by the herpes simplex viruses type 1 (HSV-1) or type 2 (HSV-2). Most genital herpes are caused by HSV-2. Most individuals have no or only minimal signs or symptoms from HSV-1 or HSV-2 infection. When signs do occur, they typically appear as one or more blisters on or around the genitals or rectum. The blisters break, leaving tender ulcers (sores) that may take two to four weeks to heal the first time they occur. Typically, another outbreak can appear weeks or months after the first, but it almost always is less severe and shorter than the first outbreak. Although the infection can stay in the body indefinitely, the number of outbreaks tends to decrease over a period of years.

Nationwide, at least 45 million people ages 12 and older, or one out of five adolescents and adults, have had genital HSV infection. Over the past decade, the percent of Americans with genital herpes infection in the U.S. has decreased.

Generally, a person can get HSV-2 infection during sexual contact with someone who has genital HSVC-2 infection. Transmission can occur from an infected partner who does not have a visible sore and may not know that he or she is infected.

HSV-1 can cause genital herpes, but it more commonly causes infections of the mouth and lips, so called "fever blisters." HSV-1 infection of the genitals can be caused by oral-genital or genital-genital contact with a person who has HSV-1 infection. Genital HSV-1 outbreaks recur less regularly than genital HSV-2 outbreaks.

Regardless of the severity of the symptoms, genital herpes frequently causes psychological distress in people who know they are infected.

If a woman has active genital herpes at delivery, a cesarean delivery is usually performed. Fortunately, infection of a baby from a woman with herpes infection is rare.

There is no treatment that can cure herpes...but antiviral medications can shorten and prevent outbreaks during the period of time the person takes the medication.

The surest way to avoid transmission of STDs is to abstain from sexual intercourse, or to be in a long-term mutually monogamous relationship with a partner who has been tested and is known to be uninfected.

HIV/AIDS

What is HIV?

HIV stands for human immunodeficiency virus. This is the virus that causes AIDS. HIV is different from most other viruses because it attacks the immune system. The immune system gives our bodies the ability to fight infections. HIV finds and destroys a type of white blood cell (T cells or CD4 cells) that the immune system must have to fight disease.

AIDS stands for acquired immunodeficiency syndrome. AIDS is the final stage of HIV infection. It can take years for a person infected with HIV, even without treatment, to reach this stage. Having AIDS means that the virus has weakened the immune system to the point at which the body has a difficult time fighting infection. When someone has one or more specific infections, certain cancers, or a very low number of T cells, she is considered to have AIDS.

HIV is a fragile virus. It cannot live for very long outside the body. As a result, the virus is not transmitted through day-to-day activities such as shaking hands, hugging, or a casual kiss. You cannot become infected from a toilet seat, drinking fountain, doorknob, dishes, drinking glasses, food, or pets. You also cannot get HIV from mosquitoes.

HIV is primarily found in the blood, semen, or vaginal fluid of an infected person. HIV is transmitted in 3 main ways...

- Having sex (anal, vaginal, or oral) with someone infected with HIV

- Sharing needles and syringes with someone infected with HIV

- Being exposed (fetus or infant) to HIV before or during birth or through breast feeding.

The only way to know whether you are infected is to be tested for HIV. You cannot rely on symptoms alone because many people who are infected with HIV do not have symptoms for many years. Someone can look and feel healthy but can still be infected. In fact, one quarter of the HIV-infected persons in the U.S. do not know that they are infected.

Once HIV enters the body, the body starts to produce antibodies—substances the immune system creates after infection. Most HIV tests look for these antibodies rather than the virus itself. There are many different kinds of HIV tests, including rapid tests and home test kits. All HIV tests approved by the U.S. government are very good at diagnosing HIV.

CDC's new Hiv/Aids Surveillance Report shows that from 2004–2007, HIV diagnoses increased 15% in the 34 states that have long-term, name-based HIV reporting.

The surest way to avoid transmission of STDs is to abstain from sexual intercourse, or to be in a long-term mutually monogamous relationship with a partner who has been tested and is known to be uninfected.

For additional material
(DVD and Leader's Guide):

www.luannebotta.com

You may view weekly devotionals there as well.